Protecting Location Privacy in the Era of Big Data

This book examines the uses and potential risks of location-based services (LBS) in the context of big data, with a focus on location privacy protection methods.

The growth of the mobile Internet and the popularity of smart devices have spurred the development of LBS and related mobile applications. However, the misuse of sensitive location data could compromise the physical and communication security of associated devices and nodes, potentially leading to privacy breaches. This book explores the potential risks to the location privacy of mobile users in the context of big data applications. It discusses the latest methods and implications of location privacy from different perspectives. The author offers case studies of three applications: statistical disclosure and privacy protection of location-based big data using a centralized differential privacy model; a user location perturbation mechanism based on a localized differential privacy model; and terminal location perturbation using a geo-indistinguishability model. Linking recent developments in three-dimensional positioning and artificial intelligence, the book also predicts future trends and provides insights into research issues in location privacy.

This title will be a valuable resource for researchers, students, and professionals interested in location-based services, privacy computing and protection, wireless network security, and big data security.

Yan Yan is a Professor of the School of Computer and Communication, Lanzhou University of Technology, China. Her research interests include, but are not limited to, privacy-preserving data collection, privacy-preserving data publishing, blockchain transaction privacy protection, and multimedia information security.

Adnan Mahmood is a Lecturer in Computing–IoT and Networking at the School of Computing, Macquarie University, Sydney, Australia. His research interests include, but are not limited to, the Internet of Things (primarily, the Internet of Vehicles), Trust Management, Software-Defined Networking, and the Next Generation Heterogeneous Wireless Networks.

Quan Z. Sheng is a Distinguished Professor and Head of School of Computing at Macquarie University, Australia. He is ranked by Microsoft Academic as one of the Most Impactful Authors in Services Computing (ranked Top 5 of All Time worldwide) and in the Web of Things (ranked Top 20 All Time).

Protecting Location Privacy in the Era of Big Data
A Technical Perspective

Yan Yan, Adnan Mahmood, and Quan Z. Sheng

CRC Press
Taylor & Francis Group
Boca Raton London New York

CRC Press is an imprint of the
Taylor & Francis Group, an **informa** business

Cover image designed by hoangpts (Shutterstock No. 2365052831)

MATLAB® and Simulink® are trademarks of The MathWorks, Inc. and are used with permission. The MathWorks does not warrant the accuracy of the text or exercises in this book. This book's use or discussion of MATLAB® or Simulink® software or related products does not constitute endorsement or sponsorship by The MathWorks of a particular pedagogical approach or particular use of the MATLAB® and Simulink® software.

First edition published 2025
by CRC Press
2385 NW Executive Center Drive, Suite 320, Boca Raton FL 33431

and by CRC Press
4 Park Square, Milton Park, Abingdon, Oxon, OX14 4RN

CRC Press is an imprint of Taylor & Francis Group, LLC

© 2025 Yan Yan, Adnan Mahmood, and Quan Z. Sheng

ISBN: 978-1-032-89988-6 (hbk)
ISBN: 978-1-032-90152-7 (pbk)
ISBN: 978-1-003-54634-4 (ebk)

DOI: 10.1201/9781003546344

Typeset in Latin Modern Roman
by KnowledgeWorks Global Ltd.

Publisher's note: This book has been prepared from camera-ready copy provided by the authors.

To my parents and my son, Leo, for their understanding, support, and love.

(Yan Yan)

To my loving wife, Fatima, and beloved children, Rafay, Talha, and Anna, for their love and support.

(Adnan Mahmood)

To my mum for her unconditional and everlasting love. To my wife, Stella, and my daughters, Fiona and Phoebe, for their love and support.

(Quan Z. Sheng)

Contents

Preface

The rapid development of the Mobile Internet and the widespread popularity of intelligent terminals have made it possible to obtain the location of users and terminals at anytime and from anywhere, thereby promoting the vigorous development of applications such as intelligent transportation, mobile group intelligence perception, and location-based services (LBS). By contributing precise location information, users and terminals can obtain location-based information recommendations and advertising placement; screen nearby medical, catering, hotel, scenic spot, bank and other life service information; understand real-time traffic operation status combining with the electronic map technology, reasonably plan travel routes, and navigate in real time.

However, big data is like a double-edged sword, which not only accelerated the development of the industry and improved data service capabilities but also brought huge challenges to personal privacy. Location data is sensitive information that can reflect users' personal privacy, the specific location of the device, and the degree of system correlation. Improper collection, analysis, and inference of location data will not only reveal the specific locations of key equipment and nodes, their roles in the system, and threaten the physical and communication security of related equipment and nodes, but also potentially lead to the leakage of privacy information such as users' home addresses, lifestyle, health status, economic conditions, social relationships, and so forth, endangering the legitimate rights and interests of users and the safety of their lives and property. Therefore, achieving privacy protection of location-based data is the primary issue that constrains the development of related businesses.

Privacy protection is a complex task that involves multiple fields. There is a risk of privacy leakage at all stages of collecting, transmitting, aggregating, publishing, and using of location-based big data. This book: analyzes the typical application fields and methods of location-based big data from its sources; summarizes the main characteristics of location-based big data; explores the possible risks to the location privacy of mobile users and smart terminals in the context of big data applications; and discusses the latest methods and effects of location privacy protection from different perspectives such as location information collection and statistical release of location-based big data. This book features case studies on three applications: location-based big data statistical publishing and privacy protection based on a centralized differential privacy model; location perturbation mechanism for the user side based on a localized differential privacy model; and terminal location disturbance based on a geo-indistinguishability model. It also shares the authors' latest ideas and insights on location privacy protection research in the era of big data, as well as future research directions.

Introduction

THE rapid development of emerging technologies such as Mobile Internet, Cloud Computing, Internet of Things, Smart Cities, Smart Homes, and the widespread popularization of intelligent terminal devices have made it possible for more and more human activities to be transformed into data and be recorded. The collection, transmission, and use of information through a large number of sensors and intelligent processing terminals not only realizes the effective connection between things and people at any time and any place but also accumulates rapidly growing data and ultimately contributes to the arrival of the big data era [1-5].

1.1 PROSPERITY OF BIG DATA TECHNOLOGY

As the cost of computing, storage, and communication has fallen exponentially, there has been an explosion in the size and variety of data. According to a report on Visual Capitalist [6], within a single minute, average 72 hours of videos will be uploaded on Youtube, 2.5 million shares will be generated on Facebook, 4 million search inquiries will be conducted on Google, 200 million emails will be sent, and 300,000 tweets will be posted. The International Data Corporation (IDC) predicts that the total amount of global data will reach 175 ZB by 2025.

The concept of "Big Data" was first formally introduced in September 2008 in a Nature's special issue, The Next Google [7]. In February 2011, Science's special issue, Dealing with Data, provided a comprehensive analysis of the "data dilemma" faced by human beings for the first time [8]. As one of the most talked-about terms in the world in the first 20 years of the 21st century, "Big Data" has not yet been defined in a uniform way, but it has been unanimously recognized in the industry as a collection of data that can't be captured, managed, and processed within a certain time frame with conventional software tools. It is a massive, high-growth, and diverse information asset that requires new processing models for greater decision-making, insight discovery, and process optimization [9].

Large volume, diverse types, rapid rate of change, and high value are the commonly recognized characteristics of big data:

- *Volume*: The first and foremost characteristic of big data is the huge volume of data. Nowadays, the magnitude of data that needs to be processed in a timely

DOI: 10.1201/9781003546344-1

manner in order to extract useful information has jumped from TB level to PB level or even EB level. With the deep application of intelligent computing devices in all areas of human work and life, the rate of data growth is increasing day by day, and the base of data is also increasing. An ordinary computer can carry out GB-level data computing in an acceptable time. Famous distributed big data processing tools such as Hadoop, Spark, Storm, etc. have been widely used. Facebook, the famous Internet company, has launched Presto, a tool that can perform EB-level real-time big data processing.

- *Variety*: Multi-source heterogeneity is a direct expression of the complexity and diversity of big data types. In addition to data with a fixed structure such as web logs and geolocation information, there are also unstructured data such as images, videos and graph data. Recently, the more popular forms of short videos, multimedia, and streaming media applications on the mobile Internet generate large amounts of unstructured data and accounting for a large proportion of big data. The unstructured and semi-structured data is what makes big data processing difficult.

- *Velocity*: The value of information lies in its timeliness. Information that exceeds a specific time frame will lose its value for use. The high-speed characteristics of big data include the need for analyzing and processing a large amount of online or real-time data, as well as the need for rapid response and no delay in inputting and extracting data. Real-time collection, transmission, processing, and distribution of big data are widely used in popular fields such as population distribution statistics, urban planning and management, intelligent transportation scheduling, disease epidemic control, and so on.

- *Value*: Big data contains inestimable value and information. Analyses, mining, and applications based on big data have attracted the attention of governments, industries, and research sectors all over the world. However, compared with the overall scale of big data, the value of individual data is very low, i.e., low value density. Only by aggregating a large amount of data for processing can valuable information be mined from it, reflecting the value of big data computing.

Big data not only implies potentially huge commercial value but is also a new tool for enhancing national governance capacity and improving public services. The application of big data for scientific analysis, prediction, and mining not only contributes to technological innovation and application development in many fields, such as social demographic surveys, public health research, urban transportation and road planning, social opinion analysis, business model investigation, agricultural yield and disease prediction, and bio-informatics analysis, but also expands the application of personal data through the openness and sharing of big data, and expands the scope and quality of social services by promoting the integration of resources. Meanwhile, the openness and sharing of big data have also expanded the application of personal data, expanded the scope, and improved the quality of social services by promoting the integration of resources [3,10-12]. The effective collaboration of big data collection, storage, and application promotes the maximization of data utility and facilitates creating a new business ecosystem. Therefore, instead of the age of information technology, we would rather say the future is the age of data technology.

1.2 FROM BIG DATA TO LOCATION-BASED BIG DATA

The development of location-aware technologies such as mobile communications and sensing devices has digitized the geographic locations of people and things. On the one hand, GPS, WiFi, and other positioning devices built into cell phones, car navigation, and other mobile devices can directly obtain the accurate location information of a mobile object at any moment and release the collected location information through various channels. For example, some new applications of mobile social networks proactively publish the location information of the user at any moment in the form of text and pictures. While personal location data is automatically and implicitly collected by the base station through the records of the user's cell phone calls, SMS, and so on. On the other hand, the acceleration, optical image, and other data collected by sensing devices such as intelligent wearable devices, which have been widely used in recent years, can also be processed to accurately determine the user's location information.

The speed and scale of location information which is automatically collected by existing sensors have far exceeded the processing capacity of information systems. According to some statistics, mobile objects such as cell phones and car navigation devices around the world submit more than several billion pieces of location information every second. In the future, developments in mobile sensing devices and improvements in communication technologies will generate location information even more frequently. In the era of big data, such a huge generation rate and data scale will bring great changes to people's lives, business operations, and scientific research. Data that contains location information and is characterized by its large size, fast generation rate, and high-value content is known as location big data.

As the natural entrance of the Internet, the real-time collection and release of location data can not only help the public to understand the state of traffic operation at any time, plan reasonable travel routes, and use real-time navigation, but also realize location-based information push, advertising, preferred nearby restaurants, hotels, attractions, banks, and other life services, etc [13-16]. According to the *Annual Research and Consultation Report of Panorama Survey and Investment Strategy on China Industry, 2023-2028* [17], the market size of China's location big data reached 9.2 billion yuan in 2021, and the proportion of the location big data market in the big data market will continue to rise in the future. The natural data value and application basis of location information in discovering laws, improving efficiency, optimizing processes, and assisting in decision-making are completely in line with the development trend of big data. With the continuous integration of new computing architecture and intelligent algorithms in the development of location information services, the use of location big data to lead the coordinated development of all links in the industry chain and improve the quality of location services will become the main direction of location information integrator in the future.

Location big data contains the characteristics of human behaviour, and its application scope involves all aspects of our work and life. If we analyze it from the three perspectives of government, enterprise, and individual, the main purpose of the application from the government perspective is to enhance the regulatory capacity and optimize public services, including social security regulation and rescue, care for special populations, and improvement of public service capacity. For example, Jana, a wireless data technology company, uses cell phone data from about 3.5 billion people to answer the major scientific questions of how diseases spread and how cities thrive, from more than 200 wireless carriers in more than 100 countries, covering Latin America, Africa, and Europe. From the perspective of enterprises, location big data applications are aimed at increasing business efficiency and reducing operational costs, such as field personnel management, precision marketing, and crisis response. For example, the United Parcel Service (UPS) has achieved great success in its business model by collecting the driving information of its own transportation vehicles to provide them with the best driving routes to reduce fuel and breakdown costs. The main purpose of location-based big data from a personal perspective is to obtain personalized services and promote information consumption, including personalized transport services based on e-map positioning, social services, e-commerce services, and other aspects based on positioning. For example, AirSage, headquartered in Atlanta, provides real-time traffic information for more than 100 cities in the United States by processing 15 billion pieces of location information from millions of cell phone users every day [18].

1.3   CHARACTERISTICS OF LOCATION-BASED BIG DATA

Location big data contains geographic and human social information that is spatially located and temporally identified. Depending on the source, location big data can be further categorized into geographic data, trajectory data, and spatial media data.

(1) Geographic data are elemental documents that represent natural and social phenomena such as geographic location and distribution characteristics, including physical geographic data and socioeconomic data. Among them, natural geographic data include land cover type, geomorphology, soil, hydrology, vegetation, settlement, river, administrative boundary, social-economic data, etc., which are generally stored according to a vector data structure or grid data structure. Social-economic data are generally in the form of statistical charts on the computer, which is the basic data for geographic analysis. Geographic data are characterized by large data volumes, relatively regular data storage, and relatively slow data change.

(2) Trajectory data is user activity data obtained by means and measurements such as GNSS, RFID, network check-in, BTS positioning, Wi-Fi, and other methods and is characterized by a large volume of data, information fragmentation, and low accuracy.

(3) Spatial media data contains media data such as digitized text-image graphics, sounds, video, and animations of spatial location and time-cause markers, which are mainly derived from mobile social networks, MicroBlogs, WeChat, and other emerging Internet applications.

Location big data accumulated by tracking and acquiring activities closely related to human life are random in nature, highly dynamic over time, and often affected by different factors such as crowds, vehicles, roads, environment, and unexpected situations. In addition to their large data volume, fast update speed, and high value, they also have the following special characteristics [19-20]:

- *Temporal correlation*: Although the total volume and update frequency of big location data change at a dynamic pace, the variation is not that huge for the adjacent data release within a certain time frame. This implies that observations at the adjacent time intervals are highly relevant. For example, a traffic congestion taking place during the morning peak hour, i.e., around 7:00 a.m., would probably last until 9:00 a.m.

- *Spatial correlation*: Combined with the distribution of urban roadside infrastructure and traffic networks, there is a certain spatial distribution pattern in the dense traffic areas of the location big data. That is, the observations gained at nearby locations are correlated with each other, subsequently leading to local coherence in space.

- *Periodicity*: Peoples' work and life follow a certain regularity; for instance, both working days and off days have alternate patterns reflected in location big data. Through the visual analysis and long-term observation of the spatial and temporal distribution, it is easy to note that there is a clear similarity among the days and between the weeks.

- *Heterogeneity*: Heterogeneity means that the contribution of different parts to the whole result is not globally the same. Location data have a heterogeneous nature both in space and time. For instance, the peak hours and rapid changes are much more important than the off-peak hours for the purpose of ensuring accurate traffic forecasting. Similarly, even within the same period of time, the densely populated commercial area is more important than the inaccessible far suburbs in terms of spatial characteristics.

- *Randomness*: Randomness primarily refers to the irregularity of location data in both time and space distribution. Although there are certain patterns in the time, place, and trajectory of people's lives and work, we still cannot accurately predict when and where users would appear or even the exact number of people in the preceding second within a certain area.

- *Uncertainty*: Uncertainty mainly refers to the unpredictability of location data. For example, owing to weather changes, traffic events, and the behaviour of traffic participants, location data may suffer fluctuations and shifts in the highest and lowest values in contrast to normal ones.

- *Diversity of data types*: Location information can be presented in numeric, textual, and graphic forms. Specifically, location can be presented in numerical form, such as latitude and longitude coordinates. It may be textual information such as street names, city names, zip codes, etc. Or it may be embedded in photos or videos posted and shared by users on social media sites.

1.4   PRIVACY RISKS IN THE ERA OF BIG DATA

Data has always been regarded as an important strategic resource because of its characteristics of processability, sharing, value-addedness, multi-use, etc. In the era of big data, the diversification of data dissemination, storage, and interaction methods may connect all the information in the digital universe into a complex data network. The correlation between such multi-source heterogeneous big data is very likely to reveal users' identities and private information, and thus promotes a brand new characteristic-data privacy [21-23].

The impact and harm of data privacy far exceed traditional data security, because even data that has met the requirements of integrity, availability, confidentiality, and reliability may suffer from linking attacks due to a change in processing method, time, place, or target of release, resulting in leakage and improper use of the data subject's sensitive information. Breaches of data privacy may jeopardize the safety and property of individuals, resulting in damage to their reputation, physical and mental health, or encountering problems such as discriminatory treatment. Data privacy in the era of big data is facing both internal and external dilemmas. Excessive and unauthorized collection of users' information, illegal use, unauthorized access, and illegal sale of personal information are the most direct causes of privacy leakage, which is also the internal dilemma of privacy protection. While data theft through system loopholes, information leakage caused by linking attacks, and the opening and sharing of data by government departments, enterprises, institutions, and individuals make the correlation of big data proliferate, resulting in the leakage of privacy as an external dilemma.

1.4.1   Risks Posed by Reckless Data Collection

In the big data era, almost all the fields related to our work and life are constantly collecting information, such as communication, medical care, socialization, travel, consumption, entertainment, and so on. The scope of the collected information includes but is not limited to general information, such as name, gender, email address, and phone number, but also contains sensitive information, such as income level, place of interest, investment status, dating information, illness and medication records, etc. When users have their information collected, they seldom have the opportunity to think about and identify who collected their data? What is the use of their data? To whom might their data have been delegated? Who will be responsible if their data is misused? Has their data been maliciously distributed online? When will their data be destroyed?

In April 2013, The New York Times reported that Apple Inc. had collected and tracked users' geographic location information through the iOS4 system on iPhones. Location information is sensitive information that can reflect users' life status, behavioural habits, and personal privacy. Through the inference and analysis of location sequences and mining, users' home address, activity trajectory, life patterns, health, and other private information can be obtained. Not coincidentally, Google Inc. was reported to track users' searching records through cookies in order to disclose users' online behaviour patterns, political tendencies, and consumption habits. All of these examples reflect the enormous privacy risks associated with the reckless collection of data and information. The existence of this type of risk is mainly due to the lack of relevant specifications for data use and supervision of laws and regulations. In order not to jeopardize users' privacy, data collection usually relies on the collector's self-consciousness and self-discipline to comply with certain norms. While in commercialized application scenarios, users have the right to choose what they want to do with their data. Users' consent must be obtained prior to the collection of personal data. Users have the right to know whether their data is shared, misused, maliciously disseminated, destroyed, and so on [24,25]. The implementation of these rights requires the construction and refinement of relevant laws and regulations on the government side.

1.4.2 Risks Associated with Data Integration

Integration and fusion of data usually employ linking operations to bring together multiple heterogeneous data sources and identify the corresponding entities. Fusion of disparate data can better serve data analysis and management. By integrating online and offline as well as sales catalogue databases, retailers can obtain more information about consumers' personal profiles and make predictions about their shopping preferences. By integrating sensor data from different segments of the road network, GPS service providers can obtain better road planning and traffic routing.

However, linking operations for integration and fusion of multiple data sources may lead to leakage of sensitive information of data entities, posing a serious challenge to personal privacy protection. Although preliminary privacy protection can be performed on each individual data source through methods such as anonymization and fuzzing, such techniques are usually more suitable for small data sources. For complex big data environments, especially when attackers possess other background knowledge, public or private data sources, they can attack the data source after anonymization or fuzzing with the help of linking attacks, which is highly likely to re-identify the personal sensitive information after anonymization, resulting in personal privacy leakage. For example, in August 2006, America Online (AOL) released 20 million search queries from 657,000 users for researchers to draw interesting insights from it. The entire database was carefully anonymized, i.e., personal information such as user names and addresses were replaced with special numeric symbols. Therefore, the researchers can link all the search queries of the same person together and analyze them without including any personal information. Nonetheless, journalists from The New York Times still identified that the user with number 4417749 is a 62-year-old widow in Georgia through a combination of background knowledge. Another example is the anonymized data from the Netflix Grand Prix released by Netflix, which was used by attackers to screen the identities of a number of subscribers through an integrated method, leading to a breach of subscribers' privacy and resulting in the cancellation of the second Netflix Grand Prix [26].

1.4.3 Risks Associated with Data Analysis

Data analysis usually includes querying, indexing, and deep knowledge discovery. Information such as anomalies, frequent patterns, classification patterns, correlations between data, and patterns of user behaviour can be obtained through data analysis, leading to serious problems such as the exposure of trade secrets or the leakage of personal privacy [27]. To a certain extent, privacy is not scary. What is scary is that user's behaviour can be predicted through big data analysis. For example, personalized recommendation systems and e-commerce websites based on big data can recommend information and commodities of interest to users based on their interest characteristics and purchasing behaviour. However, the purchase information and behavioural patterns are likely to be mined by e-commerce websites, which may lead to the leakage of private information such as income level and purchasing tendency, etc [28]. Facebook has been challenged by privacy rights organizations for tracking users' data and evaluating the effectiveness of Facebook's advertisements by analyzing such data [29].

The privacy concerns posed by big data analytics stem from three main areas: new computing frameworks, high-performance algorithms, and more complex analytical models. In the big data environment, powerful computing frameworks represented by Hadoop + MapReduce, Storm, Dremel, and R+Hadoop are able to process large-scale data in parallel with batch or streaming processing. Its performance is unmatched by traditional data mining, machine learning and online analytical processing. High-performance algorithms such as MapReduce-based k-center and k-median clustering methods, BoW multi-dimensional clustering methods, and Co-Cluster correlation clustering methods not only analyze the small, unrelated data fragments in big data, but also provide malicious analysts with conclusive background knowledge about the attacks. The emergence of more complex and efficient analytical models brings direct risks of leaking data privacy, and indirect risks of invalidating privacy protection methods, and non-erasability of analytical results. Therefore, there is a need for the emergence of data mining and machine learning methods that are more robust and privacy-preserving.

1.4.4 Risks Posed by Data Traceability

Data traceability is used to record the evolution of raw big data throughout its life-cycle (generation, collection, storage and management, processing and analysis, application and sharing, archiving, destruction), and to reproduce the historical state of the data according to the tracking path, enabling the tracing of data history records [30]. It is widely used in applications such as social networks, sensor networks, Web data fusion, data streaming, etc. Data traceability plays a critical role in accountability systems, which utilize traceability techniques to track which data have been misused and modified. However, data traceability is realized by the record information of the origin chain, but the record information itself is also privacy-sensitive data. Data owners do not want their recorded information to be accessed by operators or analyzers, nor do they want their identities to be screened. For example, in a mobile social network, Alice modifies her route to work because of her work needs. The attacker reproduces the traceability process of the historical evolution path of her trajectory data based on the information generated by Alice's movement, which then leaks Alice's many private location information. Therefore, in order to prevent malicious tampering of information related to the chain of origin in data traceability, encryption technology, authentication technology, digital watermarking, and electronic signatures are often used to protect the data traceability process.

1.5 PRIVACY PROTECTION, TECHNICAL OR POLITICAL?

Data sharing on an unprecedented scale has created enormous economic value on the one hand, and on the other hand, it has brought many controversies and hidden dangers to the whole society. Computers and the Internet have not only enabled the world to have more convenient connections, more accurate services and smarter decision-making, but have also made the public plagued by ransomware, cyber fraud, human searches, and copyright infringement. The digital age is like a panoramic prison, with surveillance and prying eyes around every corner. The non-competitive and inseparable nature of data allows it to be used over and over again without loss, and it cannot be completely divorced from the data subject. This makes it difficult to control the flow and usage of data once it is created. More and more data is being linked and integrated without being known. E-commerce companies are familiar with users' purchasing preferences. Online car rental platforms know users' travel routes. Internet companies keep users' search records. Social network software is clear about users' circles of friends and chats. All of these data reflect micro realities in various fields, and together, they paint a nuanced portrait of the individual. Private information is thus made available to the public. Personal information, which should be private, is also visible.

Literally, "privacy" is the personal information or things that are hidden, not wanted to be known, and kept secret. In 1890, American scholars, Warren and Brandeis first defined "privacy" as the right "to be alone without interference" in their book, *The Right to Privacy* [31]. Wikipedia defines "privacy" as "the ability of an individual or group to seclude themselves or information about themselves, and thereby express themselves selectively" [32]. The word "seclude" in this context implies isolation from the public sphere and confinement to private space. However, with the advent of the information age and the Internet wave, the issue of privacy has been extended from the traditional private sphere to the public sphere, which mainly refers to all kinds of information recorded electronically or by other means, can be used alone or in combination with other information, and is used to recognize the identity of a specific natural person or to reflect the activities of a specific natural person.

Driven by network and communication technologies, all kinds of digital information are disseminated, stored, exchanged, and processed in a more diversified and dynamic way on platforms such as the Internet, mobile Internet, and social networks, which results in a new form of privacy: data privacy. American scholar Westin contends data privacy as the right of individuals to control, edit, manage, and delete information about themselves and to determine when, where and in what way such information is made public [33]. In the United States, some related laws describe private data as any terms of information and record of information about an individual, including but not limited to, name, personal identification number, markings, or other special identifiers belonging to an individual (e.g., fingerprints, voice recordings, or photographs), financial transactions, medical records, criminal, or employment history, etc [34]. In the privacy-related legislation of Canada, personal information is defined as any record of information about an identifiable individual, including but not limited to, 13 categories of detailed contents, such as information about ethnicity, all kinds of identification numbers, addresses, opinions about other people, etc. Personal information protection law in Japan considers that descriptive information that can be used to identify a specific person, as well as information that can be used to refer to other information and thus identify a specific individual should be protected. According to the EU General Data Protection Regulation (GDPR) [35], "the data subjects are identifiable if they can be directly or indirectly identified, especially by reference to an identifier such as a name, an identification number, location data, an online identifier or one of several special characteristics, which expresses the physical, physiological, genetic, mental, commercial, cultural, or social identity of these natural persons".

In summary, it is not difficult to realize that the meaning of privacy varies according to countries, cultures, political environments, and legal frameworks. Privacy is a highly subjective and broad concept. Different individuals or groups have different opinions of privacy due to time, place, occupation, culture, and other factors. Even for the same individual, privacy varies with time, place, environment, life experience, and other factors. In real-world environments, privacy tends to be multidimensional, flexible and dynamic. It is also for this reason that fields such as philosophy and sociology have never come up with a clear definition of privacy during the past of more than 100 years of research, and it is very difficult to give a universal and accepted measure of privacy.

In the face of the serious problems that can result from privacy breaches, many countries have begun to enact and strengthen laws related to the protection of personal information. According to the statistics of the United Nations Conference on Trade and Development (UNCTAD), about 80% of countries globally (194 countries in total) have either completed data security and privacy legislation or have introduced draft laws as of 21st February 2022. From the *General Data Protection Regulation* of EU, to the *California Consumer Privacy Act* of the United States, and *The Data Security Law of the People's Republic of China*, and *Personal Information Protection Law of the People's Republic of China*, various countries have strengthened privacy protection and data compliance regulation to different degrees.

Nowadays, the right of privacy is recognized as a fundamental human right in many constitutions and international treaties, such as the *Universal Declaration of Human Rights*, the *International Covenant on Civil and Political Rights*, and the *American Convention on Human Rights*. The importance and protection of privacy has become a global consensus. However, relying solely on laws and regulations to protect personal privacy still has a lot of passivity and limitations. Therefore, the necessity and importance of utilizing technical methods to realize the privacy protection of data is becoming increasingly evident.

Much of the anxiety about privacy in contemporary society stems from technology's capacity for evil. At the stage of data collection, cases of inappropriate collection of personal information can be found everywhere, and the individual's right to informed consent is constantly being challenged. Generally, service providers often fulfil their obligation to inform and obtain users' consent through privacy statements according to the requirements of laws. However, most of the privacy policies are lengthy, complex and obscure. One study suggests that it would take nearly 250 hours to read all the privacy policies of the apps used in a year. At some point, these policies not only become a disclaimer for companies but also a hiding place for overbearing terms and conditions. In the absence of alternatives, users are left with no choice but to agree, and that agreement is clearly forced and formalized. To take a step back, even if the user is given a certain written undertaking, he/she can hardly verify it technically.

During the data transmission stage, there may be a series of behaviours targeting personal information, such as theft, forgery, replay, tampering, and so on. In the data storage stage, a large amount of centralized valuable data is more likely to become the target of attackers. The sources of attacks also become more diverse, and both external hackers and insiders may conspire against each other.

Privacy risks in the data use stage are facing more high-tech challenges. Although machine learning and statistical analysis are aimed at populations rather than individuals, lossy compression processing of data is not enough to defend against increasingly powerful privacy attacks in the context of arithmetic power proliferation. Machine learning models may memorize sensitive information about users. While providing too many and too precise statistics information may result in completely exposure of privacy [36]. By means of membership discrimination attacks, data reconstruction attacks, and attribute inference attacks, attackers can identify whether a given sample is present in the dataset or not, as well as recovering the value of one or some samples, and extracting information that is not included in the features or is not relevant to the learning objective [37].

In the data destruction stage, only deleting the original data itself is not sufficient to completely avoid privacy risks, as traces of personal information often remain in the data product. In addition, the deletion operation will inevitably lead to changes in system status, product performance, and so on. These changes hardly affect regular users, but can easily be detected by heavily armed attackers. They can accomplish the attack by using the similar means to the data usage stage, thus posing a threat to people's privacy.

In order to resolve the above contradiction, privacy-preserving computing technology [38] has gained wide attention in recent years, which analyzes and calculates data under the premise of privacy protection, realizing the value mining of data, and accomplishing decision-making tasks. On the one hand, privacy-preserving computing technology may protect the privacy information contained in the data, and on the other hand, it can carry out sufficient computation or processing of the data to form intelligent and precise decision-making and application, so as to realize the goals of breaking the data islands, accelerating the circulation of data, and releasing the value of data.

Privacy-preserving computing technology balances the goals of digital economy development and personal privacy protection. Wherein include both homomorphic encryption and zero-knowledge proofs based on traditional cryptography, as well as differential privacy and federated learning, which have developed rapidly in recent years. With the growing demand of data applications, privacy-preserving computing technology is also evolving and developing. The fusion and innovation of various new technologies and the cross-development of multiple disciplines are important features of the rapid development of privacy-preserving computing technologies. At the same time, privacy-preserving computing is also applied in a variety of scenarios to promote the development of digital economy.

1.6 BOOK CONTRIBUTIONS

The richly sourced location-based big data provides high-precision location services for communication equipment, transportation, aerospace instruments, robots, agricultural machinery, underwater equipment, etc., and promotes the development of applications in automobile navigation, aircraft piloting, ship ocean-going, and marine data monitoring. Various big data services based on location are widely used in popular fields such as population distribution statistics, urban planning and management, intelligent transportation scheduling, and disease epidemic control. Therefore, location-based big data and its analyzing technology have started and represented a new wave of value creation.

This book introduces the sources, characteristics, types, and application areas of location big data. It provides an insight analysis of the privacy issues arising from reckless data collection, integration, analysis, and data traceability. The current state of privacy anxiety in contemporary society is analyzed by sorting out the possible privacy risks in the life-cycle of data collection, transmission, storage, use, and destruction. In view of the privacy sensitivity of location big data and location-based services, location privacy protection technologies are classified, discussed, and compared. Typical application scenarios such as localized collection of location information and statistical release of location big data are selected, and some location privacy protection methods proposed by the authors in this field are analyzed from technical perspectives, i.e., privacy protection methods for statistical release of location big data based on the centralized differential privacy model, user-side location perturbation methods based on the localized differential privacy model, and localized location perturbation methods based on the geo-indistinguishability model.

In addition, this book shares the authors' latest thoughts and insights on location privacy protection research in the era of big data, as well as future research directions. The aforementioned will shed new light on key research issues in location privacy and facilitate the progress and development of location-based mobile applications in the future.

1.7   BOOK OUTLINE

Chapter 1 of this book begins with the fiery wave of big data, introduces the main features of big data, and focuses on analyzing location big data, the most widely used big data business today. The sources, characteristics, and privacy issues that may be raised by location big data are presented.

Chapter 2 analyses the system architecture of location-based services, their application domains and privacy protection issues. Existing methods for location privacy protection are categorized and compared in this chapter.

Chapter 3 addresses the privacy leakage problem that may be caused by the dynamic release of statistical results of location big data, introduces the differential privacy release method based on adaptive sampling and grid clustering adjustment proposed by the authors, and verifies the advantages of the proposed method in terms of the reasonableness of the moment of data release, the usability of the released data, and the operation efficiency of the algorithm through the experiments on the actual location big data set.

Chapter 4 aims at the problem of location privacy leakage on the user side that may be raised by location-based services and presents the proposed local differential privacy location protection method based on optimized random response. Experiments implemented on real location datasets demonstrate that the proposed method outperforms other methods in terms of quality loss of LBS, availability of aggregated data, and efficiency of algorithm operation.

To further improve the effectiveness of user-side location privacy protection and the quality of LBS services, Chapter 5 introduces the proposed localized location perturbation method that combines location semantics with geo-indistinguishability. Experiments and analysis on real road networks and semantic location datasets demonstrate the advantages of the proposed method over other existing location perturbation methods in terms of privacy protection strength and location data availability.

Chapter 6 summarizes the content of this book and concludes the innovations of the authors' research work in the field of location big data privacy protection. The future research hotspots of location big data privacy protection are analyzed and expected, combined with the current development trend of emerging technologies in the fields of cyberspace security and artificial intelligence.

CHAPTER 2

Location-Based Services and Location Privacy Protection

L OCATION-based service (LBS) utilizes the wireless communication network (e.g., 3G/4G/5G network) or location-aware device to obtain the current location of a mobile user, and provides various kinds of value-added service to a mobile user with the support of the geographic information system (GIS) platform [39,40]. In 1994, Schilit *et al.* [41] firstly proposed the three major contents of location-based service: "Where are you" based on spatial information, "Who are you with" based on social information, and "What resources are nearby" based on information query. Recently, the widespread popularity of mobile Internet and smart terminals has made LBS the most successful business in the field of big data applications. The wide availability and superb stitching ability of location-based big data make it a connecting bridge between the real economy and the Internet. By mining and analyzing the massive location big data, traffic information services, travel services and location services can be provided to industries such as transportation, logistics, Internet, banking, insurance, telecommunication, planning, government, and commerce. Although the commercial value realized by location big data is still a preliminary stage, the potential development space is very large.

2.1 LOCATION-BASED SERVICES

Figure 2.1 depicts the basic structure of LBS system, which is mainly composed of four parts: mobile client, positioning system, communication network, and LBS service provider. A fast and accurate positioning system is the foundation of LBS, which is also one of the most important guarantees of LBS [41]. LBS providers supply various types of services for mobile users, such as vehicle navigation, point of interest (POI) searching, and location sharing [42]. Communication networks provide the transmission medium for information interaction between mobile users and LBS providers.

 DOI: 10.1201/9781003546344-2

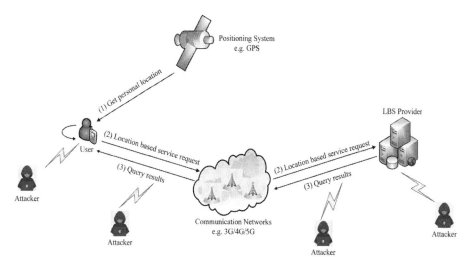

Figure 2.1 Basic structure of LBS system.

Firstly, the user obtains his or her own location information with the help of a positioning system (it is generally believed that the location information provided to the user by the positioning system is timely and accurate). Then, the user can initiate a location-based query request to the LBS provider based on his or her location and service requirements. Subsequently, the LBS provider responds to the user's query request and derives the query result through internal calculation, and finally returns the corresponding query result to the mobile client.

A typical example of an LBS application is, for example, Alice intends to go to a nearby bank and withdraw some money after finishing her visit to the hospital. She uses a mobile phone with GPS to make a query "Finding the nearest bank to my current location". The request information of this location-based service can be formalized as (*id, loc, query*). Wherein, *id* indicates the user identification of the location service request, in this case *id*=Alice; *loc* represents the location of the user when submitting the service request, in this case *loc*=(x,y) (i.e., the latitude and longitude of the current hospital where Alice is visiting); *query* is the content of the location-based request, in this case *query*=the nearest bank.

2.2 TYPICAL APPLICATION AREAS OF LBS

As emerging technologies such as new computing architectures and intelligent algorithms continue to be integrated into the development of LBS, it has become possible to effectively integrate and deeply mine massive positioning information, map information, location-associated information, and so on [43]. The potential value of LBS in discovering laws, improving efficiency, optimizing processes, and assisting in decision-making will continue to promote location big data to play an unlimited role in the fields of government administration, urban planning, and business services.

2.2.1 Government Administration

The demand for location-based services in the era of big data has entered a new stage of environmental awareness, personality needs, community behaviour monitoring and analysis, as well as comprehensive, real-time, and collaborative monitoring of geographic national conditions. LBS provides more data and tools for government administration, facilitates better understanding and responding to the needs of the public, improving the effectiveness of governance, and promoting the advancement of sustainable economic and political construction.

- *Emergency response and security management*: LBS can help governments give timely responds to emergencies such as natural disasters and terrorist attacks. By tracking and monitoring location information, the government can dispatch emergency personnel and resources to the location of an incident more accurately, improving the efficiency and effectiveness of rescue [44,45].

- *Traffic management*: LBS can help governments monitor and manage traffic flow as well as optimize the layout of road networks and traffic signals. With real-time location data, governments can better manage traffic congestion, improve road safety, and provide real-time navigation and traffic information to residents and visitors [46,47].

- *Environmental monitoring and protection*: The government can utilize LBS technology to monitor and protect the environment, such as monitoring water quality and air pollution. Through the collection and analysis of location data, the government can predict and prevent the occurrence of environmental problems and formulate relevant policies and measures to protect the environment [48].

- *Social welfare and medical services*: LBS can also be used to better understand community needs and provide personalized services and support such as educational resources, social welfare, community activities, etc. For example, during the COVID-19 pandemic, a series of location-based big data application services such as health codes, communication trip cards, and close contact self-examination programs provide great convenience for epidemic prevention and control work such as epidemiological investigations, epidemic distribution and statistical analyses, and personnel and material dispatching [49,50].

2.2.2 Urban Planning

LBS can help urban planners collect basic data from city residents and transportation in real time and efficiently, so as to understand the information on population distribution and changes, traffic flow and dense areas, and facility usage. These data can help planners better understand the current situations, needs, and trends of the city assist the government in providing guidance on comprehensive management and business support policies for target areas, make better urban planning decisions, and improve the sustainable development of the city and the quality of life of its residents.

- *Land use planning*: LBS can help planners understand the use situation of land in different areas of the city. By collecting and analyzing of location data, planners can assess the appropriate use of land and optimize land use planning, including residential, commercial, and industrial areas [51].

- *Traffic planning*: LBS, can provide detailed traffic data, including traffic flow, congestion, traffic nodes, and so on. These data can help planners understand the urban traffic situation, optimize the layout of road networks and traffic signals, improve traffic conditions, and reduce congestion [52,53].

- *Public facility planning*: LBS can help planners understand the distribution and usage of public facilities, such as schools, hospitals, and recreational facilities. By analyzing location data, planners can determine the demand and layout of public facilities to provide better services and convenience to residents [54].

- *Resident engagement and feedback*: LBS can facilitate resident engagement and feedback, helping planners better understand residents' needs and opinions. Through mobile apps and online platforms, residents can provide their location data and participate in urban planning discussions and decision-making processes [55].

2.2.3 Business Services

Location big data can be used to make horizontal comparative analyses of regional foot traffic, crowd characteristics, user preferences, etc., to accurately screen out potential customers in the neighbourhood, thus helping merchants to better satisfy users' needs, promote sales, and provide better user experiences [56,57].

- *Positioning and navigation*: LBS can provide precise positioning and navigation functions to help users find the commercial services they need, such as stores, restaurants, hotels, etc. Users can use mobile applications or navigation devices to obtain accurate location and route guidance for commercial services, improving the convenience of shopping and consumption.

- *Personalized recommendations*: LBS can provide personalized recommendations for business services based on users' location and historical data. Location-based recommendations can help businesses better understand users' preferences and needs, recommend relevant products and services to them, and improve user satisfaction and sales conversion rates [58,59].

- *Marketing and promotion*: Merchants can utilize LBS for marketing and promotional activities [60]. Special offers and discounts can be send to nearby users so as to attract them to visit the stores. LBS can also help to evaluate the effectiveness of promotional campaigns and understand users' reactions and behaviours. Advertising based on "location + user behaviour" will be the future trend of advertising. Whether it is offline advertising or mobile advertising, the best time and place for advertising can be found with the help of location big data analysis of the target group [61].

- *Business layout*: Traditional business model has not fully explored and utilized big data for business location selection. The consequence is the lack of macro view and overall layout planning for stores, no strategic decision-making supported by regional and user traffic data, and is not possible to realize systematic operation and management. However, with the help of location big data, it is possible to comprehensively compare the flow of people in each area, crowd attributes and other data to provide muti-dimensional digital support for the location of business districts, and realize the layout of selected points from the overall perspective [62].

- *Customer behaviour analysis*: The location data collected by LBS can be used by merchants to analyze and understand users' behaviour and preferences [63]. Users in different regions are profiled separately. Major users in various business districts, occupation types of users in each region, search keywords of regional users, user characteristics and preferences are analyzed. These data can be used to improve products and services, optimize merchants' marketing strategies, provide better user experience, and enhance customer loyalty.

- *Augmented reality (AR) experience*: The combination of LBS and AR technology can create rich business service experiences [64]. Location-based AR applications can be developed to provide services such as virtual tours, product displays, and interactive entertainment, which will attract users to experience and purchase.

2.3   PRIVACY IN LBS

Although LBS provide users with a full range of efficient and convenient services, users do not want their specific spatial and temporal locations to be obtained by outsiders while receiving the services, as well as the content of their query requests (especially information related to sensitive issues such as health-care, finance, and social issues), or personal information that could be inferred from their movement patterns (e.g., which roads they travel on and how often they pass through them) and interests (e.g., which shops, clubs, clinics they like to go to) [65].

2.3.1   Elements of Privacy Protection in LBS

Generally speaking, the privacy protection of LBS includes two main aspects:

(1) Protect location information, i.e., hiding the exact locations of the users. For example, users in proximity search need to submit their current locations, users in navigation services need to submit their current and destination location. Numerous studies have shown that exposing users' exact locations will lead to the disclosure of personal privacy information such as users' movement trajectories, behavioural patterns, hobbies, health conditions, and political inclinations [66,67]. In the example depicted in Section 2.1, Alice does not want people to know that she is currently located in a hospital. Because others will most likely presume that Alice or her friend/relative has some health problems based on her location. How to provide users

with the high quality of location-based services without compromising their location privacy is a key issue that constrains the further development of location-based big data, and this is the main focus of the later chapters of this book.

(2) Protect sensitive information, i.e., hiding sensitive information related to users' personal privacy. For example, inferring locations that users have visited or content of sensitive queries they have raised [68,69]. In the example depicted in Section 2.1, Alice does not want people to know that she is going to a bank. Because others are likely to infer Alice's income or consumption level based on how often she goes to a bank. In order to achieve privacy protection for sensitive content of queries submitted by users, some studies use encryption protocols to secure the query content during transmission, or with the help of enhanced encryption techniques (e.g., searchable encryption or homomorphic encryption) to enable services providers performing searching operations on encrypted query without decryption. There is also some research that removes or replaces users' identities with the help of anonymization or pseudonymization techniques, making it impossible to associate the query with a specific user. This aspect of research is beyond the scope of this book.

2.3.2 Privacy Compromising Scenarios in LBS

Location-based services not only provide great convenience for mobile users but also expose the disadvantage of location privacy leakage [70,71]. According to the system structure of LBS, the threat of privacy leakage of users exists in the following 3 scenarios.

(1) Privacy leakage on the mobile clients. If users' mobile device is captured or hijacked, it may directly lead to the leakage of users' private information on the terminals. In this case protection is provided mainly through the security mechanisms of the mobile terminal.

(2) Leakage of query requests and results during transmission in communication networks. In order to obtain more accurate query results, users often need to submit precise locations. Attackers may eavesdrop on the wireless communication environment or launch a "man-in-the-middle" attack to steal the data transmitted in the network or destroy the integrity of the data, and then obtain users' detailed information about the LBS services, including, but not limited to, the users' current locations, points of interest, and service requests. Privacy breaches in this case can be prevented by network security communication protocols, e.g. IPSec, SSL, etc.

(3) Privacy leakage on the side of LBS providers. All the locations and queries submitted by users are sent to the LBS servers, making them the major target of hackers and cyber attacks. Adversaries within the LBS system may overstep their authority to obtain users' historical records and infer private information about them by linking the records to other publicly available data. Users' historical records may even be stolen or sold to third-party organizations for profit reasons, leading to more serious privacy leakage issues. The measures for this case is more complex. Firstly, combination of technologies is needed to strengthen the security of LBS system and ensure the security of critical infrastructure such as network equipment, servers, and databases. Meanwhile, authentication and access control policies need to be strengthened to

restrict access to users' sensitive data by internal and external personnel. Regular security audits and vulnerability scans should be conducted to identify and fix security vulnerabilities in the system in a timely manner. In addition, regular security training and legal education need to be conducted for relevant practitioners.

2.3.3 Problems Caused by Location Privacy

Data is abstract, but when it corresponds to an objective point in space, it is incredibly real and concrete. Location data is quite sensitive for it can reflect the accurate location of a device, the degree of system connectivity, and personal privacy [72].

Improper collection, inference, analysis, and mining of device location may expose the exact location of critical devices and nodes. On the one hand, makes it easy to be recognized and traced by potential thieves, and the risk of equipment theft increases significantly. On the other hand, with the help of location information, the role played by relevant devices and nodes in the system can be analyzed, leading to the leakage of sensitive information such as system function, structure, and component. Finally, targeted attacks and damages launched after mastering the specific location will directly threaten the physical security and communication security of related equipment and nodes [73,74].

The high degree of adhesion between mobile smart terminals and users makes it possible to monitor users' behaviour comprehensively. Location information can not only reflect where the user has stayed, but also outline the user's trajectory of action through the linkage of time, and even speculate the user's tendency to move in the future. Improper collection, inference, analysis, and mining of users' locations may violate the privacy of individuals, leading to the leakage of private information such as users' home address, living habits, interests, health, economic conditions, social relationships, etc [75,76].

With the help of background knowledge and other publicly available data, malicious attackers may also infer users' real identities through the reckless collection and misuse of users' locations, so as to carry out targeted social engineering attacks, entice individuals to provide sensitive information, and even pose a serious threat to the personal safety of individuals and family members. It has been reported that a well-known mobile application has triggered a number of criminal cases due to its inattention to the protection of location data, which has led to the inference of sensitive locations like users' home address based on triangulation methods.

2.4 LOCATION PRIVACY PROTECTION TECHNOLOGIES

In order to achieve the privacy protection of location information, many solutions have been proposed by scholars. According to different realization principles, they can be broadly classified into the following categories.

2.4.1 Location Privacy Protection Techniques Based on Data Distortion

By allowing users to submit imprecise queries, data distortion-based approaches can prevent attackers from obtaining real information about users. For some users with less stringent privacy protection needs, this kind of technology assumes that users' location at a certain time is only related to the data collected by the attacker at the current moment. Therefore, the data distortion-based approach satisfies the intuitive privacy needs and provides a more efficient privacy protection algorithm and faster service response [77]. Randomization, spatial obfuscation, and temporal obfuscation are the mainly adopted methods. What these methods have in common is the general assumption that there has a trusted third-party server between the mobile user and the server, which can convert users' location or query into close but imprecise information before submitting to the server [78].

(1) Randomization

A randomization method was first proposed by Kido *et al.* [79], which acquires and publishes a new random location based on the previous position according to a random speed and direction. However, the movement characteristics of the historical data composed of these random generated locations may far different from those of the real moving objects. Some of the submitted locations may even be practically unreachable locations, and are easily be distinguished by attackers. Therefore, Suzuki *et al.* [80] adds constraints on mobile features such as road network and moving speed when generating random locations. Kato *et al.* [81] allows mobile objects to generate random pauses based on factors like their surroundings to further prevent attackers from distinguishing these randomly generated locations.

Another method of adding random noise to real location data is the differential privacy model [82,83]. This new and robust privacy-preserving technique, supported by mathematical theory, achieves an adjustment between the degree of privacy protection and the loss of privacy by privacy parameter ε that control the amount of noise added to the data [84]. The differential privacy model does not care about the background knowledge possessed by attackers. Even if the attacker has obtained all record information except the target record, the privacy of the target record is not compromised. This feature makes the differential privacy technique highly scaleable. Academics believe that differential privacy has a natural match with location big data. The main reason for this is that the large scale and diversity of location big data make adding or removing one location in the dataset has a very small impact on the overall data, and this trait matches the connotation of the definition of differential privacy. The specific definition and properties of the differential privacy model are given in Section 3.3 of this book.

(2) Spatial obfuscation

Spatial obfuscation satisfies the privacy protection needs by reducing the accuracy of published locations to some extent. Marco Gruteser first introduced the concept of K-anonymity in relational databases to the field of location privacy protection by proposing the location K-anonymity model [85]. This is done by generalizing the accurate location point of a user into a region containing at least K users, such that an attacker cannot obtain a precise location of a particular user. Figure 2.2 portrays the locations of seven mobile subscribers labelled as A to G at a given moment. For the purpose of location privacy protection, it is desirable that do not publish location data so accurately that only one user is included in the region. Otherwise, this user is likely to be uniquely identified. Therefore, according to the location K-anonymization

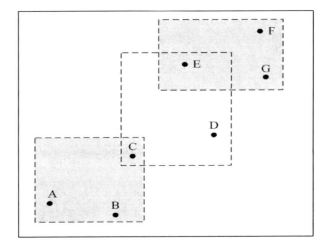

Figure 2.2 Schematic of location K-anonymity ($K=3$).

model, when publishing the location of user A or B, the shaded location anonymized region in the lower left corner can be selected (which satisfies $K=3$ anonymity). When publishing the location of user C, both the shaded location anonymized region in the lower left corner or the white location anonymized region in the middle can be selected (they all satisfy $K=3$ anonymity). The situation is the same for users E, F, and G. While for user D, when publishing his location, only the white anonymized region in the middle can be selected in order to achieve the $K=3$ anonymity.

After spatial obfuscation, each mobile subscriber sends its own location anonymized region to the LBS provider and requests for LBS service. The LBS provider needs to calculate the nearest-neighbour region that contains all the points in the location anonymized region and return the result to the user. Therefore, the first disadvantage brought by the privacy-preserving operation using spatial obfuscation is the lose of LBS service quality. Since the results of LBS services obtained based on accurate locations are more responsive to the actual needs of users. Secondly, the location K-anonymity model gives considerable assumptions on both the background knowledge of the attacker and the attack model. However, these assumptions are not fully valid in reality, and thus one can always find various ways to carry out the attack. As a result, the privacy protection based on location K-anonymity model is caught in the circle of new privacy protection mechanisms are constantly proposed but constantly broken.

(3) Temporal obfuscation

Temporal obfuscation reduces the accuracy of location data by increasing its uncertainty in the time domain. Considering that mobile objects exhibit certain characteristics in certain sensitive locations and time domains, for example, at a traffic intersection when the red traffic light is on, nearby mobile objects will have no location change for a period of time. By blurring the time domain of the location data, it can prevent the attacker from noticing the event that the user is at a traffic intersection.

TABLE 2.1   Example of temporal obfuscation for two mobile users.

Status	User	Submitted location information
Before temporal obfuscation	user 1	$< A, t_1 >, < C, t_2 >, < E, t_3 >$
	user 2	$< B, t_0 >, < C, t_1 >, < D, t_2 >$
After temporal obfuscation	user 1	$< A, [t_1, t_2] >, < C, [t_2, t_3] >, < E, [t_3, +\infty) >$
	user 2	$< B, [t_0, t_2] >, < C, [t_1, t_3] >, < D, [t_2, -\infty) >$

Table 2.1 portrays a simple example of temporal obfuscation. The first two rows depict the submitted location information of the two mobile users before the temporal obfuscation. In order to achieve the goal of location privacy protection, it is desired that the number of mobile users in each time period is not unique, since the user who appears alone in a certain period of time is likely to be identified. Therefore, the location information of the two mobile users after temporal obfuscation is shown in the last two rows of Table 2.1. Each time period obtained by the LBS provider contains at least two or more mobile users, which achieves the location privacy protection requirement of not being able to directly identify a particular user.

Location privacy protection methods based on temporal obfuscation is easy to operate and usually does not require large degree of data alteration. Therefore, it is widely used in LBS privacy protection [86]. However, with the massive and dynamic release of location big data and the increased correlation with external knowledge, the privacy preservation effect of spatial obfuscation and temporal obfuscation will degrade or even invalidate. It has been demonstrated that even if location information is generalized to 15 square kilometers and timestamps are generalized to 1 hour, it is still possible to distinguish more than 95% of users by four generalized spatio-temporal records [87].

2.4.2   Location Privacy Protection Techniques Based on Suppressed Publishing

Location privacy protection methods based on data distortion only consider whether the location at the current moment will reveal users' sensitive locations. However, users' private information may be compromised due to the temporal and spatial correlation of locations. In fact, it has been shown that the relationship between locations in time and space when a user submits a query unprotected can be portrayed by a variety of models, e.g., Hidden Markov Model [88] and Generalized Graph Model [89]. Suppression-based location privacy preservation techniques achieve location privacy preservation by not publishing sensitive location sequences that may have privacy leakage.

Gotz *et al.* [90] proposes a probabilistic speculative suppression method based on Hidden Markov Models. Aiming at the scenario that users may continuously send locations to the LBS server, the proposed method assumes that the attacker has sufficient background knowledge and speculates on user privacy for each location submitted by the user. For locations that violate privacy requirements, a probabilistic suppression release strategy is used to ensure that attackers cannot infer which sensitive location the user is located with high posterior probability.

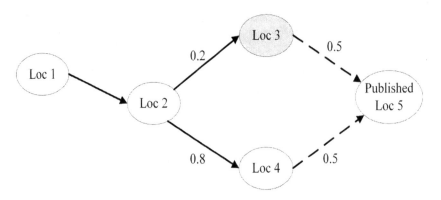

Figure 2.3 Schematic of Hidden Markov Model.

Figure 2.3 is a schematic of Hidden Markov Model established according to user's moving patterns. The user starts moving from the starting location and at subsequent moments shifts to other positions, some of which are sensitive positions (e.g., the shaded area in Figure 2.3). The probability of a user transferring between locations is determined by the parameters formed when the model was built. The prior probability that the attacker presumes that the user locates in a sensitive position is 0.2. Assuming that the location will be released with a probability of 0.5 regardless of whether the user is in a sensitive or non-sensitive location. Then, according to the Bayesian formulae, when an attacker receives the published locations with suppression, he can deduce that the user locates in a sensitive location with a posterior probability $P(A|B) = \frac{P(AB)}{P(B)} = \frac{0.2 \times 0.5}{0.2 \times 0.5 + 0.8 \times 0.5} = 0.2$. Wherein, $P(B)$ represents the probability of a user publishing his location, $P(AB)$ is the joint probability that a user publishing his location and he is in a sensitive location, and $P(A|B)$ is the probability that 'a user is in a sensitive location' occurs under the condition that 'the user publishing his location' occurs.

Use the vector $p = (p_1, p_2, ..., p_n)$ to represent the release probability of each location, where p_i denotes that the user publishes his current location i with a probability of p_i. Gradually adjusting the probability of release for each location using a greedy optimization approach. When the vector of release probability is determined, the posterior and the prior probability that the user locates in a sensitive location can be calculated according to the given trajectory using Bayesian formula and Hidden Markov Model, respectively. Determine whether p satisfies the privacy requirement based on the difference between the posterior probability and the prior probability. Keep adjusting the value of each element in p until convergence. In practice, the user's information at each location will be published according to a converged vector of publishing probabilities.

The Hidden Markov Model assumes that the next publishing location is only relevant to user's current location. Such an assumption facilitates the efficient creation of the model, but the calculation of the probability that a user locates in a certain location at a certain moment is not very accurate. Considering that historical data also implies whether the user's current location is sensitive or not, historical data also has a great impact on whether the current location can be safely published. Komishani *et al.* [91] proposed a privacy-preserving algorithm to support sensitive attribute generalization and local suppress. The algorithm determines the spatio-temporal sequence of suppressed locations according to the different needs of users for the strength of location privacy preservation, and employs the sequence suppression and sensitive attribute generalization decision tree for spatio-temporal suppression of the sensitive locations. Terrovitis *et al.* [92] proposed four trajectory anonymization algorithms based on global suppression, local suppression, trajectory segmentation, and hybrid suppression and segmentation for the problem of record association attack. They pointed out that the algorithm of trajectory segmentation and hybrid suppression and segmentation are more capable of guaranteeing the subsequent practicability of the location data through comparative experiments. Lin *et al.* [93] proposed a trajectory privacy protection algorithm that combines global suppression and local suppression with pruning strategy.

The advantages and disadvantages of suppression-based location privacy preservation techniques are very distinct. For the evaluated insensitive location spatio-temporal sequences, the method allows the submission of the user's real location and query content, so that the quality of the obtained LBS service is higher than that of the data distortion-based location privacy preservation technique. For the sensitive location spatio-temporal sequences obtained from the evaluation, the suppression-based approach directly drops them out, resulting in the absence of this part of data and sacrifices the usability of the LBS application. Therefore, the user cannot receive an effective LBS services at the suppressed spatio-temporal locations.

2.4.3 Location Privacy Protection Techniques Based on Data Encryption

The above two types of location privacy protection techniques achieve location privacy protection by publishing distorted locations and suppressing the publication of location data. However, these two types of methods cannot meet the requirements of users with high privacy needs. Data encryption-based location privacy protection technology utilizes encryption algorithms to encrypt users' query contents (including location attributes, sensitive semantic attributes, etc.) and sends them to the LBS service provider. The LBS service provider performs direct query processing based on the received data without decryption. The query result returned to the client by the service provider needs to be decrypted by the user according to his private key and the final query result can be obtained. In this process, the service provider cannot get the specific content of the user's query because it does not have the key. The service provider cannot even grasp the meaning of the query result returned to the client [94,95].

(1) Anonymous communication networks

Anonymous communication networks use encryption techniques and intermediate nodes to hide the location information of the sender and receiver of the communication [96]. One of the most famous anonymous communication networks is the onion router network (Tor) [97]. The core idea of Tor is to protect the privacy of users' communication through multi-hop proxies and layers of encryption. Users' data is encrypted multiple times as it passes through the Tor network. Each node of the

Tor network can only decrypt one layer of encryption, just like peeling an onion. Therefore, users' anonymity has been guaranteed. In terms of privacy protection, Tor hides users' real IP address, making it impossible for the target server to track users' location. Users' data is encrypted as it passes through the Tor network, providing an additional layer of security. Tor makes users' identities more difficult to trace over the network, as the attacker would need to break through multiple layers of encryption to reveal users' identities.

(2) Secure multi-party computation

Secure multi-party computation aims at solving the problem of collaborative computation for privacy preservation among a set of mutually distrustful participants [98,99]. Generally speaking, a secure multi-party computation problem computes any probability function based on any input over a distributed network. Each party has an input on this distributed network. The distributed network has to ensure that the inputs are independent, computationally correct, and do not reveal any information other than their respective inputs that can be used to derive other inputs and outputs. The strategy to solve the above problem is to assume that there is a trusted service provider or a trusted third party. However, in the current volatile and hostile environment, this is extremely risky. Therefore, protocols that can support joint computation and protect the privacy of participants become increasingly important. With secure multi-party computation, multiple participants can aggregate and analyze location data without revealing their individual locations.

(3) Homomorphic encryption

Traditional cryptography schemes focus on data storage security. When the two participants of communication want to send or store information, they need to encrypt the data before sending and storing. The use of encryption algorithms ensures that in the process of data transmission and storage, even if it is accessed by other people, it will not disclose the real content of the data, that is, to achieve the visibility and unavailability of the data. The concern of homomorphic encryption, on the other hand, is data processing security. It provides a capability to process the encrypted data, which means that other people can process the encrypted data without revealing any of the original content in the process [100]. The decryption after complete data processing will obtain the results of the same processing on the original data. In other words, the data is available but not visible.

Homomorphic encryption makes it possible to perform calculations on encrypted data, which means that data processing can be outsourced to a third party without trusting the third party to properly protect the data [101,102]. Because without the correct decryption key, the original data is inaccessible. In recent years, data breaches and hacking attacks on large websites and cloud platforms have resulted in record financial losses and adverse impacts. The ability of processing encrypted data via homomorphic encryption allows organizations to outsource critical data processing with minimal risk and protect against these supply chain risks. In LBS services that incorporate homomorphic encryption, users can encrypt sensitive information such as their locations and query contents and submit them to the location service provider, who will realize the query service in ciphertext, effectively protecting users' location privacy and query privacy.

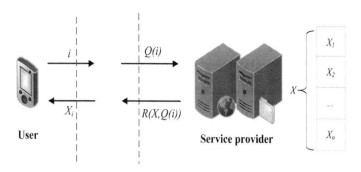

Figure 2.4 Information retrieval process based on PIR.

(4) Private information retrieval (PIR)

PIR is a secure protocol for client-server communication, which ensures that the query is completed and the query result is returned under the condition that the client's private information is not disclosed to the server [103,104]. As depicted in Figure 2.4, the user wants to get the content at location i on the server database from the service provider. The user himself encrypts the query request to get $Q(i)$ and sends it to the service provider. The service provider finds X without knowing i, encrypts the result $R(X, Q(i))$ and returns it to the user, who can easily compute X_i. In the PIR-based location privacy preservation technique, the server of the service provider cannot obtain the location of the mobile user and the specific object to be queried. Thus preventing the server from obtaining users' locations, as well as determining users' points of interest and inferring their privacy information based on the object queried by the user. While during the communication between the client and the server, attackers cannot get i by parsing the eavesdropping or intercepted packets. Therefore, they cannot obtain the location of the querying user and the content of his query.

2.4.4 Performance Evaluation and Summary

Location privacy-preserving technologies need to protect users' location privacy while balancing usability and overhead. Generally, the performance of location privacy protection technology can be measured from the following aspects.

- *Service availability*: which refers to the accuracy and timeliness of the published location information. It can reflect the location-based service quality available to users after privacy-preserving processing.

- *Privacy protection degree*: usually reflected by the disclosure risk of the privacy-preserving technology. There is a mutual constraint between service availability and the degree of privacy protection. Increasing the level of privacy protection tends to reduce the availability of services.

- *Overhead*: including the storage and computational costs incurred at both pre-computation and execution. The storage cost mainly occurs at pre-computation. With the continuous upgrading and updating of modern computer equipment,

TABLE 2.2   Comparison of location privacy protection technologies.

Techniques	Protection degree	Execution cost	Computation cost	Data loss
Distortion-based techniques	Medium	Medium	Low	Medium
Suppression-based techniques	Mid-to-high	Low	High	Medium
Encryption-based techniques	High	High	High	Low

the cost in this area is usually acceptable and is ignored when choosing privacy protection technologies. The computational cost during execution is generally measured using the time complexity of CPU computation time as well as the number of file block accesses. This part of cost mainly depends on the characteristics of the location big data privacy-preserving technology.

Location privacy-preserving techniques have different characteristics. Table 2.2 analyses and compares various existing privacy protection techniques from different aspects. When the required location privacy protection degree and the computational overhead are high, the suppression-based privacy protection technique is more suitable. When perfect location privacy protection is concerned, the encryption-based location privacy protection techniques can be considered. Such methods are more costly in terms of computation and response time. Distortion-based location privacy protection technique can achieve the protection of general privacy needs with low computational overhead.

CHAPTER 3

Dynamic Statistical Publishing and Privacy Protection of Location-Based Big Data via Adaptive Sampling and Grid Clustering

To realize dynamic statistical publishing and privacy protection of location-based data, this chapter proposes a differential privacy publishing algorithm based on adaptive sampling and grid clustering and adjustment. The PID control strategy is combined with the data variation difference to realize the dynamic adjustment of data publishing intervals. The spatial-temporal correlations of the adjacent snapshots are utilized to design the grid clustering and adjustment algorithm, which facilitates saving the execution time of the publishing process. The budget distribution and the budget absorption strategies are improved to form the sliding window-based differential privacy statistical publishing algorithm, which realizes continuous statistical publishing and privacy protection and improves the accuracy of published data. Experiments and analysis on large datasets of actual locations show that the proposed privacy protection algorithm is superior to other existing algorithms in terms of the accuracy of adaptive sampling time, availability of the published data, and execution efficiency of data publishing methods.

3.1 INTRODUCTION

According to some surveys, more than 80% of the big data in the real world are related to geographical location [105]. Statistical analysis and mining of location-based

DOI: 10.1201/9781003546344-3

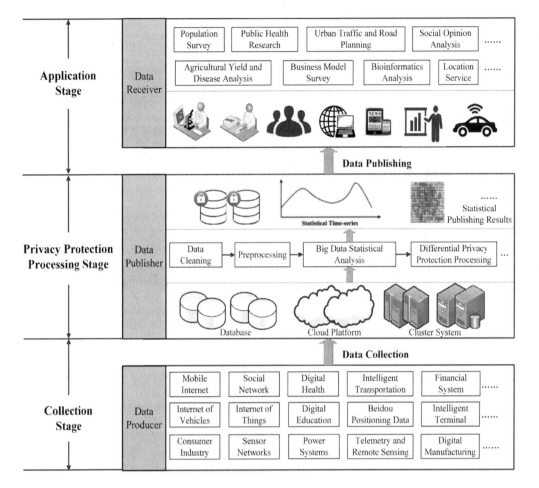

Figure 3.1 Statistical publishing framework of location-based big data using differential privacy.

big data have been widely used in social population surveys, public health investigation and prediction, traffic and road planning, social public opinion analysis, business model investigation and adjustment, and many other fields [106-108]. Figure 3.1 depicts the statistical publishing framework of location-based big data using differential privacy. In practical applications, the dynamic statistical publishing of location-based big data needs to solve the following problems.

(1) Reasonable sampling intervals should be selected to release statistics of location-based big data. The traditional approach adopts a fixed time interval sampling method. For example, various vehicles with positioning systems may report their locations to respective data centers at regular intervals; traffic flow monitoring stations usually release statistical results of nearby traffic flow every few minutes. The significant issue with this method is that if the time interval is too large, the published data may miss the actual maximum or minimum period of traffic flow. In some serious cases, it will seriously damage the validity of location-based services. For example, users will miss the best time to take a bus. When the time interval is

too small, the amount of storage, operation, and computation required for publishing data will sharply increase, leading to unnecessary resource waste.

(2) Spacial partition structure will affect the accuracy of published statistics of location-based big data. Traditional statistical publishing method of location-based data mainly adopts the top-down partitioning process to construct grid-based or tree-based partitioning structures, which is prone to "over-partitioning" or "under-partitioning". The unreasonable partition structure increases the noise error and uniform assumption error of differential privacy statistical publishing, leading to a decrease in the accuracy of published results. For example, according to the location statistics, the actual number of COVID-19 patients in a city is 11,650. However, the published result is 10,075 according to the traditional grid-based partition structure combined with differential privacy noise, which may lead to the insufficient distribution of drugs and medical equipment for some patients.

In order to address the above problems, this chapter proposes a differential privacy-preserving publishing method based on adaptive sampling and grid clustering and adjustment. The main contributions are as follows:

- To better reflect the dynamic change process of the real data in the published results, an adaptive sampling mechanism is proposed by combining the PID control strategy. The sampling interval is dynamically adjusted by comparing the data change difference between adjacent publications as well as the difference between the real value and the predicted value. The proposed sampling algorithm is normalized by the Pearson correlation coefficient, which can be applied to more scenarios.

- To improve the execution efficiency of the statistical publishing process, a grid clustering and adjustment algorithm is designed according to the spatial-temporal correlation of data within adjacent publishing times. By clustering and merging neighbourhood grids, there is no need to perform complex partitioning and clustering processes at all the publishing times, which saves lots of running time for the statistical publishing algorithm.

- To provide privacy protection for the continuous publishing process of location-based data, a sliding window-based differential privacy protection algorithm is proposed. The budget distribution (BD) and budget absorption (BA) strategies are improved to allocate a reasonable differential privacy budget for w consecutive publishing moments so that the published data falling within the sliding window can maintain the same differential privacy protection strength.

3.2 STATE OF THE ART

In order to realize the privacy protection of location information, researchers have proposed various solutions such as location anonymity, suppression, encryption, and perturbation. Gruteser first introduced the concept of K-anonymity in relational databases into the field of privacy protection for location services and proposed the location K-anonymity model [85]. In order to achieve location K-anonymity, some algorithms generalize the user's accurate location into an area containing at least K users [109,110]. While other algorithms use a large number of fake locations including the real one to form the K-anonymity area [111,112]. Although the above algorithms can protect the precise location of the user from being leaked, they drop the quality of location-based services significantly. Data publishing privacy protection technology based on suppression algorithm [113,114] prefers to delete sensitive information in the data according to the user's specific requirements for privacy before publishing. Compared with other methods, the publishing privacy protection algorithm that suppresses sensitive information has the least computational overhead. However, suppressed data records or sensitive information will lead to the loss of data and affect the accuracy of published data. The privacy protection method based on cryptography [115,116] encrypts and transmits sensitive information (e.g., location) so that attackers do not have the decryption key and cannot obtain valid data about sensitive information. However, cryptography algorithms are computationally and communication expensive, and require additional mechanisms for key management and negotiation. Perturbation-based location privacy protection technology adds random noise to real data [117,118] or implements a perturbation strategy for location semantics [119], which can better balance accuracy of published data on the basis of privacy protection.

Partition and clustering are two effective ways to achieve the statistical publishing of location-based big data. The partition and publishing algorithm implements privacy spatial decomposition on the location-related space and incorporates random noise into the statistical results to achieve differential privacy protection. Yang *et al.* [120] improves the traditional quadtree partition structure and proposes a partitioning algorithm based on location density. The area is recursively divided into four sub-units according to the maximum density difference. The hierarchical differential privacy hybrid decomposition strategy (HDPHD) proposed by Yan *et al.* [121] first performs adaptive grid partition according to the density distribution of the locations, and then sets two density thresholds to divide the grid into three types, and adopts adaptive grid partition or heuristic quadtree partition for different density types of grids. Their proposed method effectively improves the accuracy of published data. Yan *et al.* [122] proposes an unbalanced quadtree partition and publishing algorithm using regional uniformity as the judgment condition. The proposed method traverses the sub-trees according to the depth-first strategy and performs quadtree iterative partition adaptively according to the uniformity. The spatial decomposition algorithm proposed by Rodriguez *et al.* [123] extracts the optimal spatial decomposition from the statistical information of the spatial distribution of particles, so that each unit includes uniformly distributed particles in space. The location privacy protection scheme proposed by Wei *et al.* [124] uses a three-level adaptive grid partition structure and an adaptive complete pyramid grid algorithm to split the location of mobile crowdsourcing services into noisy grids.

Clustering spatially adjacent data is not only conducive to improving the accuracy of statistical publishing data but also can protect the location information corresponding to a single record. For location information, the clustering algorithms often use grid-based or density-based clustering methods [125,126]. Since the calculation of the distance between grids is small, it has high clustering efficiency. The location data clustering algorithm proposed by Cai *et al.* [127] can deal with unbalanced datasets with large density differences, find clusters generated by minority data, and reduce the time complexity of the clustering process. The big data statistical information publishing algorithm proposed by Yan *et al.* [128] combines grid partition with clustering. It first divides the 2D space into uniform grids to realize the calculation of big data statistical information. Then, the uniformity of the non-empty grids is judged and the uniformly distributed grids are classified by the wavelet decomposition algorithm. Finally, clustering and Laplace noise addition are performed on the neighbourhood similarity grid within the same density level, which improves the accuracy of statistically published data.

In the research aspect of big data dynamic statistical publishing and privacy protection, Fan *et al.* [129] propose a framework for real-time aggregated statistical information publishing based on differential privacy filtering and adaptive sampling, which not only publishes the data of sampling points but also predicts and releases the data of non-sampling points. The PID adaptive sampling algorithm proposed by Yan *et al.* [130] adjusts the publishing interval according to the amount of updated data, which solves the shortcomings of fixed time interval sampling. The real-time trajectory data differential privacy protection mechanism designed by Ma *et al.* [131] uses an integrated Kalman filter based on the location transition probability matrix to predict the data, and combines regional privacy weights to allocate privacy budgets, ensuring the privacy and availability of real-time vehicle trajectory data. Iqbal *et al.* [132] proposes an adaptive sliding window algorithm based on deep learning, which dynamically limits the size of the sliding window to capture the latest trends in resource utilization. Ahsani *et al.* [133] and Sayed *et al.* [134] improve the CluStream algorithm and use sliding windows for clustering respectively. The resulting model is updated only with the latest data and old data is dropped, resulting in faster execution and better results.

3.3   PRIOR KNOWLEDGE

The differential privacy model is a privacy protection method based on data perturbation. It has a rigorous mathematical definition and can quantitatively analyze the degree of privacy protection. The main principle of differential privacy is to protect users' privacy by adding random noise to the statistical results of the original data and removing individual characteristics on the premise of preserving the statistical characteristics of the dataset. The differential privacy model does not need to establish special attack assumptions. By adding random perturbations to the published data, the attacker cannot identify whether a certain tuple is in the original data in the statistical sense, no matter what background knowledge he has. As a research hotspot of privacy protection technology, the differential privacy model has a natural match with the location-based big data statistical publishing application. This is because of the large scale and dynamic change of location-related big data, which makes the impact of adding or deleting certain data in the dataset very small on the

TABLE 3.1   Mathematical notations.

Symbol	Description
ε	Privacy budget
K	A random algorithm
$\triangle f$	Sensitivity
$S_{t_i} = \{D_{t_1}, ..., D_{t_i}\}$	Prefix dataset of snapshots D_{t_i} on continuous time stamps t_i
m	Partitioning granularity of the 2D plane
N	The total number of grids after partition
Min_count	The minimum number of users within a grid
Max_count	The maximum number of users within a grid
$Predict\_value$	The predicted statistics number of users within a grid
FE_i	Feedback error for publishing time t_i
$Pearson(a, b)$	Pearson correlation coefficient between a and b
φ	PID statistical error
D_P, D_I, D_D	Proportional gain, integral gain, and derivative gain
T_I	The integration time window
DS_i	Dynamic data sequence between publishing time t_i and t_{i-1}
DR_i	Data variation difference
I, I_0, I_{new}	The Initial sampling interval, the minimum sampling interval, and the dynamic sampling interval
$Den(G)$	The density of grid G
ρ	Uniformity threshold
CSS_i	Cluster structure similarity
μ, γ	Different thresholds for clustering structural similarity
CSM_{t_i}	Cluster structure matrix of current time t_i
GC_{t_i}	The number of non-empty grids on current time t_i
GDC_{t_i}	Number of grids with changes in density level
w	Length of the sliding window
AE	The average error
$y_i, \hat{y}$	The original and published statistics
$RE(q)$	The relative error of range counting query on q
$C(q), C^*(q)$	The real statistical results and the published statistical results of query range q

whole, which is very consistent with the connotation of the definition of differential privacy.

Before detailing the dynamic statistical publishing and privacy protection methods proposed in this chapter, we first provide an introduction to the definition of the differential privacy model and its implementation. To facilitate the understanding of subsequent definitions and descriptions, Table 3.1 provides a unified explanation of the mathematical notations defined and employed in this paper.

3.3.1   Differential Privacy

Definition 3.1 *ε-Differential privacy [82,83]: For any output $Y \subseteq Range(K)$, if the random algorithm K obtains the same output result on any pair of sibling datasets D_1 and D_2 (only have one different record), the probability satisfies the following* *formula:*

$$P_r[K(D_1) \in Y] \le e^{\varepsilon} \times P_r[K(D_2) \in Y] \tag{3.1}$$

Then, the algorithm K satisfies ε-differential privacy.

The definition of ε-differential privacy provides strong protection on the published data that the presence or absence of an individual will not significantly affect the output of a query. Even if an attacker gets all the other data except a specific target record, it is still impossible to infer whether the target record exists in the original data, thus achieving privacy protection for user data. The privacy budget ε determines the strength of privacy protection. The smaller the value of ε, the higher the privacy protection degree provided by the algorithm K.

Definition 3.2 *Sensitivity [135]: For any pair of sibling datasets D_1 and D_2, and the query mapping function f, the sensitivity $\triangle f$ is expressed as the maximum L_1-norm distance between the outputs of the query mapping function on D_1 and D_2:*

$$\triangle f = max_{D_1, D_2} ||f(D_1) - f(D_2)||_1 \tag{3.2}$$

For location-based big data statistical publishing applications, the sensitivity of statistical publishing results is $\Delta f = 1$.

Theorem 3.1 *Serial combination property* [136]: For a set of random algorithms $\{K_1, K_2, ..., K_n\}$ acting on the same dataset D, where K_i ($1 \le i \le n$) satisfies ε_i-differential privacy on the dataset D, then the set of random algorithms $\{K_1, K_2, ..., K_n\}$ can achieve ε-differential privacy for the dataset D, wherein $\varepsilon = \sum_{i=1}^{n} \varepsilon_i$.

Theorem 3.2 *Parallel combination property* [136]: If the dataset D can be divided into multiple independent and disjoint subsets $\{D_1, D_2, ..., D_n\}$, a set of randomized algorithms $\{K_1, K_2, ..., K_n\}$ acting on the above subset respectively, where K_i ($1 \le i \le n$) satisfies ε_i-differential privacy for the data subset D_i, then the set of random algorithms $\{K_1, K_2, ..., K_n\}$ can achieve $max\{\varepsilon_i\}$-differential privacy for the dataset D.

3.3.2 Laplace Mechanism

Definition 3.3 *Laplace mechanism [135]: For numerical data, the Laplace mechanism achieves differential privacy protection by adding a small amount of independent noise to the output of the query mapping function f. Let $f(D)$ be the result obtained by the query mapping function on the original dataset D, the query result returned by the Laplace mechanism can be expressed as $K(D) = f(D) + \eta$. Where η is a continuous random variable that satisfies the Laplace distribution, and its probability density function can be expressed as:*

$$P_r[\eta = x] = \frac{1}{2b} e^{-\frac{|x-\mu|}{b}} \tag{3.3}$$

Combined with the definition of sensitivity, the incorporated independent noise obeys the zero-mean Laplace distribution with magnitude $b = \frac{\triangle f}{\varepsilon}$. Figure 3.2 portrays the distribution characters of Laplace function.

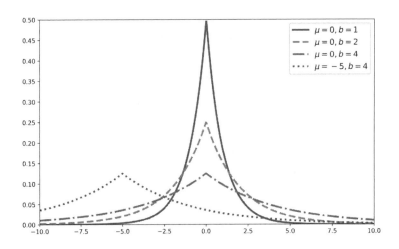

Figure 3.2 Probability density function of the Laplace function.

3.3.3 (w, ε) Window-Level Differential Privacy

Definition 3.4 *Prefix dataset [137]: The collection of data snapshots on continuous time stamps is referred to as a prefix dataset. For example, if the dataset at timestamp t_1 is D_{t_1}, the dataset at timestamp t_2 is D_{t_2}, ... the dataset at timestamp t_i is D_{t_i}, then, the set $S_{t_i} = \{D_{t_1}, D_{t_2}, ..., D_{t_i}\}$ is called a prefix dataset.*

Definition 3.5 *w Nearest neighbour [137]: For two prefix datasets S_{t_i} and S'_{t_i}, within any window length w, if there are two datasets D_{t_i} and D'_{t_i} at each corresponding moment in S_{t_i} and S'_{t_i} are identical or adjacent datasets, then S_{t_i} and S'_{t_i} are said to be w nearest neighbours.*

Definition 3.6 *(w, ε) Window-level differential privacy [137]: If the output set of the random algorithm K for two w nearest neighbour datasets S_{t_i} and S'_{t_i} is Y, and the algorithm K satisfies ε differential privacy, then the algorithm K is said to satisfy (w, ε) window-level differential privacy.*

$$P_r[K(S_{t_i}) \in Y] \leq e^{\varepsilon} \times P_r[K(S'_{t_i} \in Y] \tag{3.4}$$

3.4 DYNAMIC DATA PUBLISHING BASED ON ADAPTIVE SAMPLING

The location-based data distribution exhibits a particular spatial-temporal correlation when combining road distribution and population movement characteristics in real life. Due to the user's mobility speed, location-based data statistics will not create significant changes during neighbouring publishing times. This section proposes an adaptive sampling approach for dynamic statistical publication by combining the data variation difference between adjacent publishing times with the PID control strategy. Figure 3.3 portrays the process of the proposed dynamic adaptive sampling method.

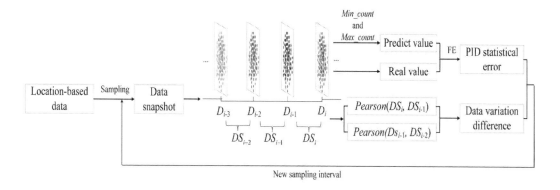

Figure 3.3 Process of the proposed dynamic adaptive sampling method.

Firstly, the flat area covered by location-based data can be partitioned into $m \times m$ independent grids of equal size. For each publishing time, the real number of users located in each grid can be calculated. Then, the statistical number of users for each grid at the next release time can be predicted based on users' moving speed. There are two extreme cases: if only users move outside the original grid during the two consecutive publishing times and no external users enter the grid, then the number of users in this grid achieves the minimal value, represented as Min_count. On the other hand, if only users enter the grid during the two consecutive publishing periods and no internal users depart the grid, the maximum number of users, represented by Max_count, will be reached.

Definition 3.7 *Predicted value: Let Max_count and Min_count be the maximum and the minimum number of users for the same grid respectively. The average value of Max_count and Min_count can be used to represent the predicted statistics number of users within the grid at the next publishing time.*

$$Predict\_value = \frac{Max\_count + Min\_count}{2} \qquad (3.5)$$

Definition 3.8 *Feedback error: For any publishing time t_i, let RC and PC be the real and predicted statistical values for the partitioned area x, respectively. Then, the feedback error can be expressed as:*

$$FE_i = 1 - |Pearson(RC, PC)| \qquad (3.6)$$

$$Pearson(a, b) = \frac{1}{N-1} \sum_{x=1}^{N} \left(\frac{a_x - \bar{a}}{\sigma_a}\right)\left(\frac{b_x - \bar{b}}{\sigma_b}\right) \qquad (3.7)$$

wherein the Pearson correlation coefficient is used to measure the correlation between the real and the predicted statistical value, N is the total number of grids after partition on the published data, $\bar{a}$ and σ_a are the mean value and standard deviation of a_x respectively, $\bar{b}$ and σ_b are the mean value and standard deviation of b_x respectively.

Definition 3.9 *PID statistical error: The PID statistical error combines all the factors from proportional error, integral error, and derivative error, which can be expressed as:*

$$\varphi = D_p \times FE_t + \frac{D_I}{T_I} \times \sum_{j=N-T_I+1}^{N} FE_j + D_D \times (FE_t - FE_{t-1}) \qquad (3.8)$$

wherein D_P, D_I, and D_D are the proportional gain, integral gain, and derivative gain respectively, satisfying $D_P, D_I, D_D > 0, D_P + D_I + D_D = 1$. D_I represents the integral gain, T_I is the integration time window, FE_t and FE_{t-1} are the feedback errors at adjacent publishing times.

Definition 3.10 *Data variation difference: Let DS_i be the dynamic data sequence between publishing time t_i and t_{i-1}, and DS_{i-1} be the dynamic data sequence between publishing time t_{i-1} and t_{i-2}, a series of dynamic data sequences can be received similarly. Data variation difference can be defined as the difference in correlations between adjacent data series:*

$$DR_i = Pearson(DS_i, DS_{i-1}) - Pearson(DS_{i-1}, DS_{i-2}) \qquad (3.9)$$

wherein the Pearson correlation coefficient is used to measure the correlation of adjacent dynamic data sequences. The closer the Pearson coefficient value is to 1, the better the correlation between dynamic data sequences. Therefore, if the statistical results of consecutive adjacent published data change from obvious fluctuations to relatively flat, there is $DR > 0$. In this case, it can be considered to increase the sampling time interval to save unnecessary computational and storage costs. On the contrary, if the statistical results of consecutive adjacent published data change from relatively flat to obvious fluctuations, there is $DR < 0$. In this case, the sampling time interval should be shortened so that the statistical results of the published data can better reflect the actual process of data changes.

Combining the PID control strategy with the data variation difference at the publishing time of adjacent samples, a dynamic sampling interval adjustment scheme is proposed as follows:

$$I_{new} = max\{I_0, I \times [e^{\theta - \varphi} + (e^{DR} - 1)]\} \qquad (3.10)$$

wherein I represents the initial fixed sampling time interval. To avoid an excessively small sampling time interval, we predetermined the minimum sampling interval I_0. Considering that it is not necessary to repeatedly publish highly similar statistical results in a short period, we set $I_0 = 5s$ in this chapter. The value of the minimum sampling interval I_0 can also be adjusted according to the needs of some specific application scenarios.

Algorithm 3.1 describes the detailed implementation process of the proposed dynamic adaptive sampling algorithm. Lines 1-4 obtain the data snapshot at the publishing time and the dynamic data sequence between publishing times according to the initial fixed sampling time interval. Lines 5-9 perform uniform grid partition on the snapshot and obtain the real statistical and predicted number of users in each grid. Lines 10-15 calculate the new sampling interval according to the proposed algorithm and obtain the corresponding data snapshot.

Algorithm 3.1 Dynamic adaptive sampling algorithm

Input: Incoming dataset D, the original fixed sampling interval I, minimum sampling interval I_0, partition granularity m, parameter θ

Output: Snapshot dataset SD; new sampling interval I_{new};

1: $t_1 = 0, t_2 = I, t_3 = 2I, t_4 = 3I$
2: **while** the amount of incoming data $\neq 0$ **do**
3:     Snapshot dataset $SD \leftarrow$ select data from D within time interval $[t_2, t_3]$
4:     Data sequences $DS_1, DS_2, DS_3 \leftarrow$ get the amount of data at each time from D within time interval $[t_1, t_2], [t_2, t_3]$ and $[t_3, t_4]$
5:     Partition the 2D area of SD into $m \times m$ uniform grids
6:     **for** each grid **do**
7:       Get the real number of users
8:       Get the predicted number of users according to Eq. (3.5)
9:     **end for**
10:     Get FE according to Eq. (3.6) and Eq. (3.7)
11:     Get φ according to Eq. (3.8)
12:     Get DR according to Eq. (3.9)
13:     Get I_{new} according to Eq. (3.10)
14:     $t_1 \leftarrow t_2, t_2 \leftarrow t_3, t_3 \leftarrow t_2 + I_{new}, t_4 \leftarrow t_3 + I$
15:     return SD and I_{new}
16: **end while**

The new sampling time interval is determined by two aspects: $e^{\theta - \varphi}$ is the sampling interval adjustment part based on PID statistical error, and $(e^{DR} - 1)$ is the sampling interval adjustment part based on the data variation difference at adjacent publishing times. Wherein, φ is the PID statistical error, and DR is the data variation difference. We set the parameter $\theta = 0.5$. Because when the predicted value of the statistical results is closer to the real value, the feedback error is smaller, resulting in a smaller proportional error, and φ has a closer valve approach to 0. In this case, the value of $\theta - \varphi$ will be larger, and the corresponding adjustment of the sampling interval will be greater. On the contrary, when the predicted value of the statistical results varies significantly from the real value, the feedback error will be large, resulting in a higher proportional error, and φ has a closer valve approach to 1. In this case, the value of $\theta - \varphi$ will be smaller, and the effect is to reduce the sampling interval.

3.5 GRID CLUSTERING AND ADJUSTMENT FOR THE STATISTICAL PUBLISHING OF LOCATION-BASED DATA

The statistical publishing process of dynamic big data conforms to typical time series characteristics. New generated or updated data between adjacent publishing moments constitute a data snapshot. Partition data snapshot is an effective way to realize the

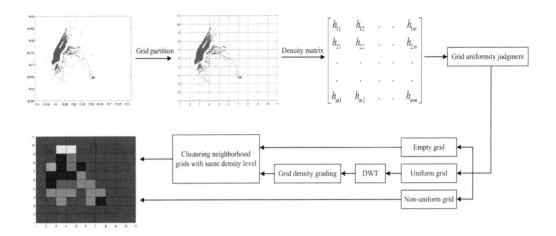

Figure 3.4 Process of the statistical publishing method based on grid clustering.

publishing of location-based big data statistics. It first decomposes the 2D plane covered by location information into grids or tree, and then counts and releases data such as the number of users, the number of queries, and hot events according to the partition structure. An intuitive solution for realizing the above location-based dynamic big data partition and publishing is to use the same static data partition and publishing algorithm for all the data snapshots. In order to solve the "over-partitioning" and "under-partitioning" problems of the traditional partition and publishing algorithm, we proposed a statistical publishing algorithm based on grid clustering [128]. The main process of this algorithm is portrayed in Figure 3.4, which first divides the 2D area into equal-sized sub-grids and calculates the number of users within each grid to get the density matrix. Then, the sub-grids are classified into different types after grid uniformity judgment. Finally, the neighbourhood grids with the same density level will be aggregated respectively to get the final statistical publishing structure.

Although the above-mentioned grid clustering method can be used to obtain the statistical publishing structure for data snapshots at all publishing times, the disadvantage of this scheme is that there is a large number of redundant calculations. Figure 3.5 depicts the statistical publishing structures of adjacent publishing times acquired by using the above-mentioned grid clustering method. It is obvious to find that the distribution of location-based data does not change a lot at adjacent publishing times, and their statistical publishing structures are quite similar. As portrayed in Figure 3.5 (b) and (d), the publishing structures of adjacent publishing time t_{i-1} and t_i only differs in three sub-grids (marked as 1, 2, and 3). Combined with the distribution characteristics of location information, the statistical results of big data at adjacent publishing times have high spatial-temporal correlations [138,139].

Although location-based big data is constantly updated and changed, statistical changes within adjacent publishing times are always within a certain range due to movement speed and other factors. The distribution characteristics of location-based statistical results also have certain spatial redundancy. Therefore, a grid clustering and adjusting algorithm is proposed for the statistical partition and publishing of

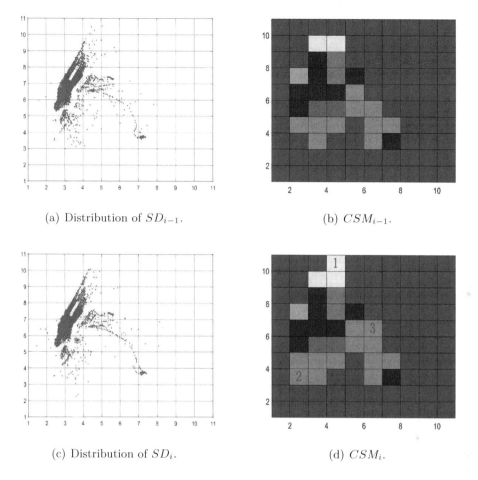

(a) Distribution of SD_{i-1}.　　　　　(b) CSM_{i-1}.

(c) Distribution of SD_i.　　　　　(d) CSM_i.

Figure 3.5　Statistical publishing structures at adjacent publishing times.

continuous data snapshots. Combined with the dynamic adaptive sampling process proposed in Section 3.4, the proposed algorithm compares the statistical partition structures at adjacent publishing times to make appropriate adjustments in areas with similar partition structures without performing the same grid clustering process at all the publishing times.

Definition 3.11 *Grid uniformity: For a grid G with a density of $Den(G)$, let D_1, $D_2, ..., D_i$ be the density of the sub-regions of grid G partitioned from horizontal, vertical, diagonal, and other directions (as portrayed in Figure 3.6). If a row vector $V = \{D_1, D_2, ..., D_i\}$ is constructed, then the distribution uniformity of the grid G can be represented by the variance $Var(V)$ of vector V. If the following Eq. (3.11) is satisfied, the grid G is said to be a uniformly distributed grid.*

$$|log_{10}(Var(V)) - log_{10}(\frac{Den(G)}{i})^2| \le \rho \qquad (3.11)$$

wherein, ρ is the uniformity threshold, i is the number of sub-regions after multi-directional segmentation.

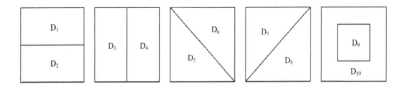

Figure 3.6 Multi-directional segmentation schematic.

Definition 3.12 *Grid density grading: Let LL be the low-frequency coefficients of the original grid density matrix after the 2D DWT transform, $\overline{LL}$ is the mean value of the coefficients. The original grid density matrix can be classified into three levels:*

$$Class(i,j) = \begin{cases} 1 & if \quad LL(i,j) \leq \frac{1}{3}\overline{LL} \\ 2 & if \quad \frac{1}{3}\overline{LL} < LL(i,j) \leq \frac{2}{3}\overline{LL} \\ 3 & if \quad \frac{2}{3}\overline{LL} \leq LL(i,j) \end{cases} \quad (3.12)$$

Definition 3.13 *Cluster structure similarity: Let $GC_{t_{i-1}}$ be the number of non-empty grids in the grid density matrix at the last publishing time t_{i-1}, and GDC is the number of grids with changes in density level between publishing time t_{i-1} and t_i. Cluster structure similarity at the current publishing time t_i can be defined as follows:*

$$CSS_i = \begin{cases} H & if \quad \frac{GDC}{GC_{t_{i-1}}} < \mu \\ M & if \quad \mu \leqslant \frac{GDC}{GC_{t_{i-1}}} < \gamma \\ L & if \quad \gamma \leqslant \frac{GDC}{GC_{t_{i-1}}} \end{cases} \quad (3.13)$$

wherein μ and γ are the thresholds for the similarity of the cluster structure. $CSS_i = H$ indicates that the similarity of the cluster structures of adjacent publishing times is extremely high. In this case, the current publishing time can be skipped to save the computing and storage resources. If $CSS_i = M$, it means that the similarity of cluster structures at adjacent publishing moments is relatively high. Therefore, the grid clustering and adjustment algorithm needs to be implemented. While if $CSS_i = L$, it means that the similarity of the cluster structures at adjacent publishing times is low. It is necessary to restart the grid partition and clustering algorithm [128] on the current data snapshot.

The grid clustering statistical partition and publishing algorithm [128] requires judging the uniformity of each grid during the clustering process. It reduces the noise error by merging the neighbourhood uniform grids of the same level and restricts the quality loss of published data caused by uniformity assumption error. However, judging the uniformity of all the grids cost a huge calculation overhead, which slows down the operation efficiency of the original grid clustering algorithm. In order to solve the above problems, the statistical publishing structure adjustment algorithm proposed in this section simplifies the uniformity judgment process by comparing the grid density levels at adjacent publishing times. If the grid density level remains unchanged, the uniformity of the grid is believed to have no changes. Otherwise, the uniformity of the grid needs to be judged. Finally, different types of neighbourhood grids are clustered and merged to form the statistical publishing structure.

Algorithm 3.2 Grid clustering and adjustment algorithm

Input: Snapshot dataset D_{t_i} of the current time, partition granularity m, uniformity threshold ρ, cluster structure matrix $CSM_{t_{i-1}}$ for the last publishing.

Output: Cluster structure matrix CSM_{t_i} of the current time, the number of non-empty grids GC_{t_i} of the current time, the number of grids with changes in density level GDC_{t_i} of the current time.

1: Partition the 2D area of snapshot dataset D_{t_i} into $m \times m$ uniform grids
2: $GC_{t_i} \leftarrow$ calculate the number of non-empty grids
3: **for** each grid $(i,j)_{1 \leqslant i,j \leqslant m}$ **do**
4:    $Den_{t_i}(i,j) \leftarrow$ calculate the density of current grid
5: **end for**
6: Complete DWT transform on Den_{t_i} and classify the non-empty grid into different levels according to the Definition 3.12
7: $CSM_{t_i} = CSM_{t_{i-1}}$
8: Initiate $GDC_{t_i} = 0$ to represent the number of grids whose density level has changed
9: **for** each grid $(i,j)_{1 \leqslant i,j \leqslant m}$ **do**
10:    Compare the density level of the current grid at adjacent moments t_{i-1} and t_i using $CSM_{t_{i-1}}$
11:    **if** its density level is changed **then**
12:       $GDC_{t_i} = GDC_{t_i} + 1$
13:       Perform grid uniformity judgment according to Eq. (3.11) and mark the result in CSM_{t_i}
14:    **else**
15:       Mark the current grid as a uniform grid in CSM_{t_i}
16:    **end if**
17: **end for**
18: $CSM_{t_i} \leftarrow$ Merge neighbourhood empty grids and uniform grids with the same density level respectively [128]
19: return $CSM_{t_i}, GC_{t_i}, GDC_{t_i}$

Algorithm 3.2 depicts the detailed process of grid clustering and adjustment algorithm proposed in this section. The definition of concepts such as grid uniformity, neighbourhood grid, and grid density grading are consistent with those defined in [128]. Lines 1-6 of the algorithm perform uniform grid partition and density statistics on the 2D area covered by the dataset and classify all the non-empty grids according to their density. Lines 7-17 compare the grid density level at adjacent publishing times to obtain the uniform grids with unchanged density levels and judge the uniformity of the other grids. Lines 18-19 merge the neighbourhood uniform grids and empty grids into clusters respectively, and return the final statistical partition and publishing structure. Figure 3.7 depicts a schematic diagram of the grid clustering and adjustment on data snapshots at adjacent publishing times.

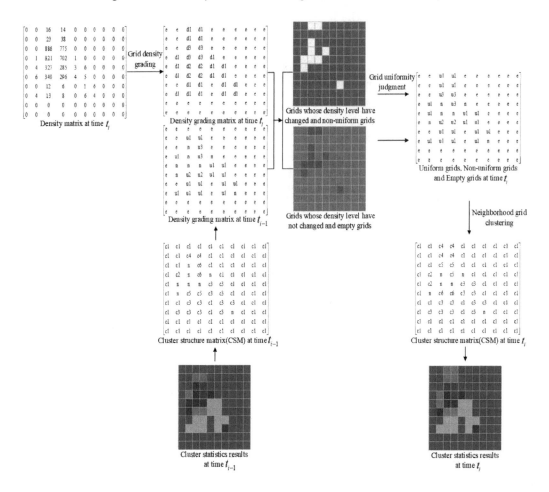

Figure 3.7 Grid clustering and adjustment on data snapshots at adjacent publishing times.

3.6 DIFFERENTIAL PRIVACY PROTECTION ALGORITHM FOR CONTINUOUS DATA PUBLISHING BASED ON SLIDING WINDOW

Numerous applications require continuous publication of location-based big data statistics, such as real-time traffic analysis, disease transmission monitoring, and population mobility survey. The publishing process of the above-mentioned application is actually an infinite stream of data snapshots published periodically. Differential privacy model for such data stream can be mainly classified into *event-level* and *w-event level*. The *event-level* differential privacy model proposed by Dwork *et al.* [140] achieves perturbation by allocating the same privacy budget ε for the stream data or time-series data at each publishing moment. In order to ensure the balance of privacy and accuracy of infinite stream data, Kellaris *et al.* [137] proposed the *w-event level* differential privacy model. By allocating the privacy budget ε over the data in w windows, the *w-event level* model can provide differential privacy protection for sequence data in continuous time windows of arbitrary w length.

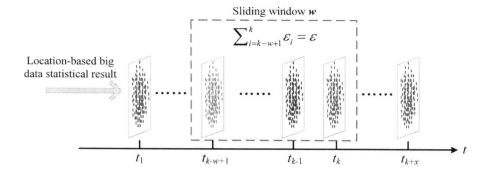

Figure 3.8 The example of privacy budget allocation.

In most of the location-based practical application scenarios, sensitive information such as users' locations, places of interest, and moving trends can be revealed from multiple events occurring at contiguous time instances. Therefore, it is necessary to provide differential privacy protection for location-based big data statistics in any continuous time or window range. We take advantage of the *w-event level* differential privacy model and propose a sliding window-based differential privacy protection algorithm for the statistical publishing of big data. The privacy budget is allocated to w consecutive data publishing moments of location-based big data statistical results (as shown in Figure 3.8) so that arbitrary publishing data within the sliding window maintains the same differential privacy protection strength as time goes on.

Combined with the dynamic adaptive sampling algorithm proposed in Section 3.4 and the grid clustering and adjustment algorithm designed in Section 3.5, the proposed sliding window-based differential privacy protection algorithm (as portrayed in Figure 3.9) will first compare the clustering structure similarity between the data snapshots at the current sampling moment and the nearest publishing results. If $CSS_i = H$ according to Eq. (3.13), the last publishing results will be used for the current moment (i.e., no new location-based big data statistical results will be published) to save the consumption of differential privacy budget. Otherwise, the privacy budget will be allocated for the current data snapshot using an improved budget distribution (BD) or budget absorption (BA) method. Laplace noise will be incorporated into the statistical results after grid clustering and adjustment to achieve (w, ε) *window-level* differential privacy.

The improved BD method allocates the privacy budget in two stages: the first stage allocates a fixed proportion of the privacy budget for each publishing moment, as expressed in Eq. (3.14); the second stage allocates the remaining privacy budget within the sliding window in an exponentially decreasing manner for the published data snapshots, as depicted in Eq. (3.15). The total privacy budget at each publishing moment is $\varepsilon_i = \varepsilon_{i,1} + \varepsilon_{i,2}$. For the publishing moment that has slipped out of the window, the consumed privacy budget is recovered for subsequent use.

$$\varepsilon_{i,1} = \frac{\varepsilon}{2w} \tag{3.14}$$

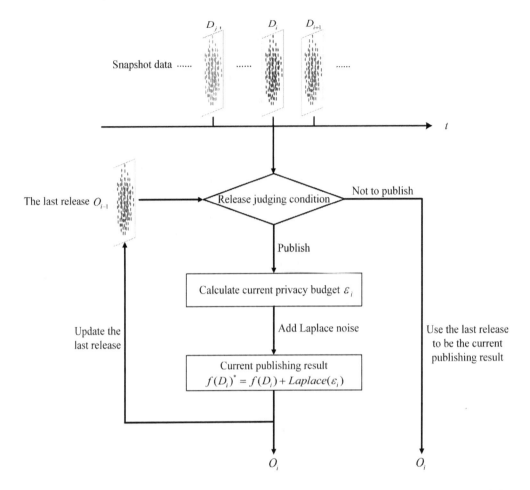

Figure 3.9 Process of the differential privacy publishing algorithm based on sliding window.

$$\varepsilon_{i,2} = \begin{cases} \dfrac{\dfrac{\varepsilon}{2} - \displaystyle\sum_{k=i-w+1}^{i-1} \varepsilon_{k,2}}{2} & \text{for} \quad \textit{publication time} \\[4mm] 0 & \text{for} \quad \textit{non-published time} \end{cases} \qquad (3.15)$$

The improved BA method also allocates the privacy budget in two stages. In the first stage, a fixed proportion of the privacy budget is allocated to each publishing time according to Eq. (3.14). In the second stage, the remaining privacy budget in the sliding window is also allocated to each publishing time at a fixed ratio, but for the non-publishing time, the privacy budget will be combined and assigned to the subsequent publishing time, as shown in Eq. (3.16). While the second-stage privacy budget at the next moment after the absorption occurs will be set to 0. The total privacy budget at each publishing moment is $\varepsilon_i = \varepsilon_{i,1} + \varepsilon_{i,2}$.

$$\varepsilon_{i,2} = \begin{cases} \frac{\varepsilon}{2w} & \text{for} \quad \textit{publication time} \\ \frac{\varepsilon}{2w} \times 2 & \text{if} \quad D_{i-1} \textit{ don't published} \\ 0 & \text{for} \quad \textit{non-publication time} \end{cases} \tag{3.16}$$

Algorithm 3.3 Differential privacy protection algorithm based on sliding windows

---

Input: Privacy budget ε, cluster structure similarity threshold μ and γ, window length w

Output: Publish statistical result based on grid O_i

1: Get SD and t_i according to Algorithm 3.1
2: **for** each publication time t_i **do**
3:   **if** $t_i = 1$ **then**
4:     Get CSM_{t_i} and GC_{t_i} according to the grid clustering algorithm [128]
5:   **else**
6:     **if** $CSS_i = M$ **then**
7:       Get CSM_{t_i}, GC_{t_i} and GDC_{t_i} according to Algorithm 3.2
8:     **else if** $CSS_i = L$ **then**
9:       Get CSM_{t_i}, GC_{t_i} and GDC_{t_i} according to algorithm [128]
10:     **end if**
11:     Get CSS_i according to Definition 3.13
12:   **end if**
13:   $O_i = 0$
14:   **if** $CSS_i \neq$ H or $t_i=1$ **then**
15:     $n \leftarrow$ Calculate the number of clusters in CSM_{t_i}
16:     $\varepsilon_i \leftarrow$ Calculate privacy budget of the current publishing according to Eq. (3.14), Eq. (3.15), and Eq. (3.16)
17:     **for** each cluster **do**
18:       $u \leftarrow$ Get the number of grids within the current cluster
19:       $sum\_Den \leftarrow$ Sum the density of grids belonging to the same cluster
20:       $noisy\_sum = sum\_Den + Laplace(\frac{S}{\varepsilon_i})$
21:       $O_i = noisy\_sum/u$
22:     **end for**
23:   **else**
24:     $O_i = O_{i-1}$
25:   **end if**
26:   $O_{i-1} = O_i$
27:   return O_i
28: **end for**

Algorithm 3.3 depicts the pseudo-code of the differential privacy protection algorithm based on sliding windows. Line 1 calls Algorithm 3.1 to determine the publishing time and obtain a snapshot of the dataset at that moment. Lines 3-12 compute the cluster structure similarity for the current time of publication via Algorithm 3.2

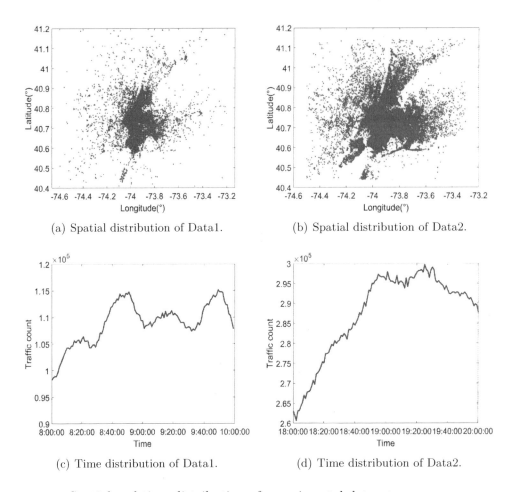

(a) Spatial distribution of Data1.

(b) Spatial distribution of Data2.

(c) Time distribution of Data1.

(d) Time distribution of Data2.

Figure 3.10 Spatial and time distribution of experimental datasets.

or the grid clustering algorithm [128]. Lines 14-25 incorporate Laplace noise into the statistical results according to the improved privacy budget allocation methods. Lines 26-27 save and release the statistical results at the time of publication.

3.7 EXPERIMENTAL AND ANALYSIS

This section will compare the results of the proposed dynamic statistical publishing and privacy protection method with other existing algorithms in terms of the accuracy of adaptive sampling time, the performance of the grid clustering and adjustment algorithm, and the effectiveness of sliding window privacy budget allocation. The experimental datasets are drawn from the 2015 New York TLC Trip Record Data dataset [141]. We select records from two rush hours (8:00 - 10:00 and 18:00 - 20:00) to create two location-based datasets, Data1 and Data2. The spatial and temporal distributions of the experimental datasets are depicted in Figure 3.10.

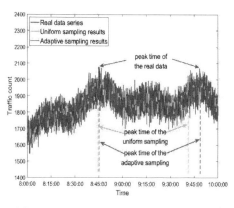

(a) Different sampling effects on Data1.

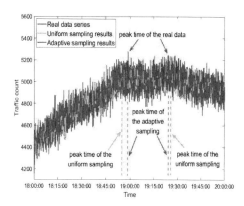

(b) Different sampling effects on Data2.

Figure 3.11 Comparison of different sampling algorithms.

3.7.1 Adaptive Sampling Effect on Location-Based Data

In order to verify the adaptive sampling effect of the proposed algorithm, we compare it with the traditional scheme of fixed time intervals. Parameter settings for the experiments are $D_P = 0.9$, $D_I = 0.1$, and $D_D = 0$. The reason for setting a smaller value of integral gain is to control the PID statistical error φ within $(0,1)$, which is convenient for the calculation of the new dynamic sampling time interval. In addition, although the differential error can control the future state of the system, it is not easy to implement. Therefore, we set the differential gain to be 0 and directly compare the actual changes of data in adjacent periods to control the future sampling interval more intuitively. The fixed sampling interval is set to be $I = 15s$, $\theta = 0.5$, and the minimum sampling interval is set to be $I_0 = 5s$ to prevent the sampling interval from being 0.

Figure 3.11 compares the results of the proposed adaptive sampling algorithm with the traditional uniform sampling method. In Figure 3.11(a), the traditional uniform sampling method gets 300 samples, and the proposed adaptive sampling algorithm gets 296. In Figure 3.11(b), the number of samples is 300 and 295, respectively. It can be observed that when the sampling times are roughly the same, the changing trend of the traditional method has no obvious relationship with the fluctuation of statistical data. While the curve of the proposed adaptive sampling algorithm is closer to that of the real statistical data. In $Data1$, the peak times of the real data appear at 8:44:52 and 9:48:26. The traditional uniform sampling method captures the peak times at 8:44:48 and 9:41:12. While the proposed adaptive sampling algorithm captures the peak times at 8:45:00 and 9:48:47. In $Data2$, the real peak times appear at 18:58:43 and 19:23:56. The results of the traditional uniform sampling method appear at 18:54:48 and 19:25:36. While for the proposed adaptive sampling algorithm, the peak times appear at 18:58:47 and 19:23:56. It can be concluded that the proposed adaptive sampling algorithm can better capture the dynamic changes in the published data.

3.7.2   Performance of Spatial Partition Algorithms

To evaluate the performance of the proposed grid clustering and adjustment algorithm, it is compared with some up-to-date partition methods, including but not limited to, the density-based quadtree partition algorithm (DBP) [120], hierarchical differential privacy hybrid decomposition algorithm (HDPHD) [121], unbalanced quadtree partition algorithm (UBQP) [122], adaptive three-level grid decomposition algorithm (ATGD) [124], and the simple grid clustering statistical publishing algorithm (GCDPP) [128].

3.7.2.1   Accuracy of Published Statistical Data

This section uses average error to evaluate the accuracy of published statistical results of various spatial partitioning algorithms on the experimental datasets. For the sake of fairness, all the comparison algorithms use the same initial partition granularity and take privacy budget $\varepsilon = 0.1$ as an example. The average error of published statistical results is defined as follows:

$$AE = \frac{\sum\limits_{i=1}^{N} |y_i - \hat{y}_i|}{|D|} \tag{3.17}$$

wherein N is the total number of grids after partition, y_i represents the original statistics within each region, $\hat{y}_i$ denotes the published statistics of the corresponding region, and $|D|$ is the size of the dataset.

Figure 3.12 compares the average error of various partition algorithms on different datasets. To be fair, all the partition algorithms use the same dynamic adaptive sampling method proposed in this chapter (i.e., Algorithm 3.1) and receive the same data snapshots at the release times. It can be observed from Figure 3.12 that among all the comparison algorithms, the average errors of HDPHD and ATGD are significantly higher than other algorithms, DBP and UBQP take the second place.

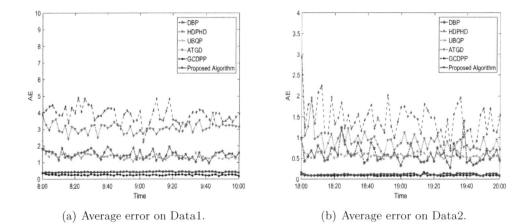

(a) Average error on Data1.   (b) Average error on Data2.

Figure 3.12   Comparison of average error on different datasets.

TABLE 3.2   Experimental datasets and query range.

Parameters	subData1	subData2	subData3	subData4
Data amount	21726	39833	24522	38052
Location range	$[40.4°\mathbf{N} \sim 41.2°\mathbf{N}, -74.5°\mathbf{W} \sim -73.1°\mathbf{W}]$			
Querying range (longitude×latitude)	q1: $0.02° \times 0.015°$ q2: $0.04° \times 0.03°$ q3: $0.08° \times 0.06°$ q4: $0.16° \times 0.12°$ q5: $0.32° \times 0.24°$ q6: $0.64° \times 0.48°$			

Although the average error of the proposed grid clustering and adjustment algorithm is slightly inferior to that of the GCDPP algorithm, it is significantly better than others. The primary reason is that the GCDPP algorithm performs the same grid partitioning and clustering operations on each data snapshot, thus obtaining more accurate statistical structures at all data publishing times. while the proposed grid clustering and adjustment algorithm only makes local adjustments to areas with high similarity in statistical publishing structures at adjacent data publishing times, rather than re-executing complete grid partitioning and clustering operations. Therefore, the statistical publishing structure of the proposed algorithm is not as accurate as the GCDPP algorithm, but it can save more running time than the GCDPP algorithm (will be discussed later).

3.7.2.2   Accuracy of Range Counting Query

This section uses relative error to evaluate the accuracy of range counting queries on the published statistical data. Adjacent data snapshots, $subData1$ and $subData2$ are randomly selected from $Data1$, $subData3$ and $subData4$ are randomly selected from $Data2$. Specific information is depicted in Table 3.2. During the experiment, the maximum density difference of the DBP algorithm is set to be $\beta = 5$, the privacy distribution ratio of the HDPHD algorithm is $\alpha = 0.5$, the partitioning depth of the UBQP algorithm is $h = 6$, and the partition granularity is set to be $m = 80$ for the ATGD algorithm, the GCDPP algorithm and the proposed algorithm, cluster structure similarity threshold $\mu = 0.2, \gamma = 0.5$. The definition of relative error can be expressed as:

$$RE(q) = \frac{|C^*(q) - C(q)|}{max\{C(q), \rho\}} \tag{3.18}$$

wherein q represents the area of range counting query, $C(q)$ is the real statistical results within query range q, and $C^*(q)$ is the published statistical results within query range q. To prevent the denominator from being zero, set $\rho = 0.001 \times |D|$, and $|D|$ represents the size of the dataset.

Figure 3.13 to Figure 3.16 compare the relative errors of range counting queries for various spatial partition algorithms on different datasets and different privacy budgets. The abscissa uses different sizes of queries set in Table 3.2 and the ordinate uses logarithmic results to represent the relative error under different query sizes.

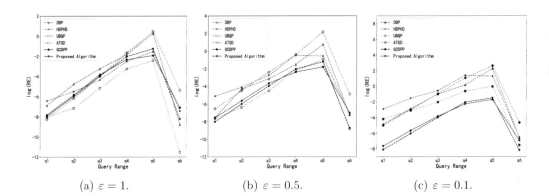

(a) $\varepsilon = 1$.   (b) $\varepsilon = 0.5$.   (c) $\varepsilon = 0.1$.

Figure 3.13 Comparison of query accuracy of subData1.

Observing the above results, it can be found that the relative errors of various spatial partition algorithms at adjacent moments are not much different. On the same dataset, the relative errors of various spatial partition algorithms increase as the privacy budget ε decreases. This is mainly because the reduction of the privacy budget ε in the differential privacy model will increase the Laplace noise, increasing the gap between the statistical value of the noisy published results and the real statistical value, thereby increasing the relative error. On all the datasets, as the increase of query range, the overall trend of relative error first increases and then decreased. The reason is that when the query range is small (such as q1 and q2), the range covered by the query only includes a small number of spatial units, and the added noise interference is small, so the error with the real statistical results is also limited. When the query range is large (such as q5 and q6), the range covered by the query is closer to the root node in the partition index structure, and the uniformity assumption error introduced is small, so the relative error is also reduced.

In a specific comparison of various spatial partition algorithms, it can be found that when the privacy budget ε is large, the relative errors of all the algorithms have little difference. This is primarily because the larger the privacy budget value is, the smaller the added Laplace noise will be, which reduces the relative error caused by

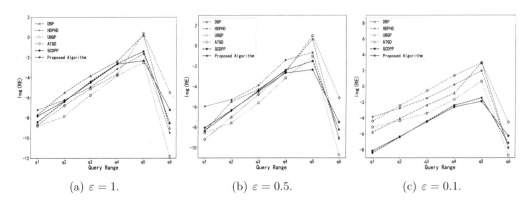

(a) $\varepsilon = 1$.   (b) $\varepsilon = 0.5$.   (c) $\varepsilon = 0.1$.

Figure 3.14 Comparison of query accuracy of subData2.

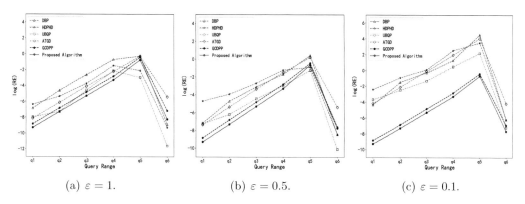

(a) $\varepsilon = 1$.　　　　　　(b) $\varepsilon = 0.5$.　　　　　　(c) $\varepsilon = 0.1$.

Figure 3.15　Comparison of query accuracy of subData3.

adding noise. However, with the decrease in the privacy budget value, the advantages of the GCDPP algorithm and the proposed algorithm are gradually obvious. The proposed algorithm adjusts the clustering structure according to the spatial similarity based on the GCDPP algorithm. It can be observed from the above figures that the proposed algorithm maintains good accuracy of published data just like the GCDPP algorithm.

3.7.2.3　*Execution Time for Constructing the Partition Structures*

This section compares the execution time of various algorithms in constructing partition structures on the experimental datasets. For the sake of fairness, all the comparison algorithms use the same dynamic adaptive sampling method proposed in this chapter (i.e., Algorithm 3.1) and receive the same data snapshots at the release times. The parameter settings of various algorithms keep the same as those previously. Since the differential privacy budget has no significant impact on the execution time of different partition algorithms, we take $\varepsilon = 0.1$ as an example to compare the execution time of consecutive publishing moments.

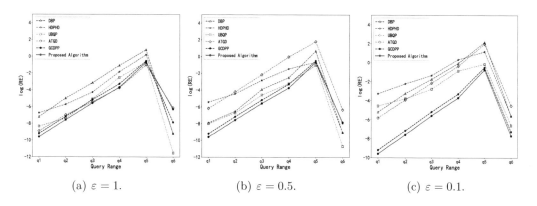

(a) $\varepsilon = 1$.　　　　　　(b) $\varepsilon = 0.5$.　　　　　　(c) $\varepsilon = 0.1$.

Figure 3.16　Comparison of query accuracy of subData4.

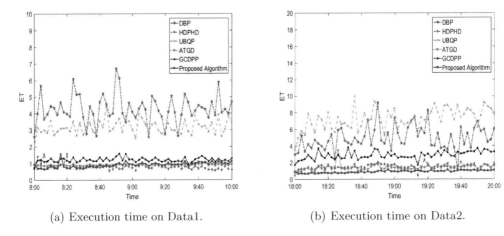

(a) Execution time on Data1.

(b) Execution time on Data2.

Figure 3.17 Comparison of execution time on different datasets.

It can be observed from Figure 3.17 that the DBP and UBQP algorithms take more time to construct the partition structures on each data snapshot. The reason is that the partition process of these two algorithms is related to the spatial distribution of the location-based dataset and partition depth of the quadtree. For a location-based dataset with n records and h partition depth, the time complexity of these two algorithms will be $O(hn)$ in the worst case. The HDPHD algorithm adopts the adaptive density grid decomposition in the first layer to prevent "over-partitioning" in empty areas. In the second layer, the heuristic quadtree partition and adaptive grid partition are used in different types of first-layer grids. The overall time complexity of the HDPHD algorithm is approximately $O(n + n^2) \approx O(n^2)$. However, because the distribution of experimental datasets in dense areas is rather homogeneous, unwanted heuristic quadtree partitioning is avoided. As a result, the HDPHD algorithm consumes less execution time than other algorithms during the experiments. To construct a three-level adaptive grid partition structure, the ATGD algorithm has to scan the input data three times. The time complexity of the ATGD algorithm is $O(3n)$. The GCDPP and the proposed algorithm first perform the uniform grid partition and then merge the neighbourhood grids of the same type and density grade to generate the clusters. These two algorithms have a time complexity of $O(n + n) \approx Q(2n)$. Our proposed algorithm spends equal time with the GCDPP algorithm on the publishing moment requiring complete grid clustering. While on the other publishing times, it only makes local adjustments to areas with high similarity in statistical publishing structures. Therefore, the overall efficiency of the proposed algorithm is the best among all the algorithms, as depicted in Table 3.3.

3.7.3 Comparison of Privacy Budget Allocation

To verify the advantages of the improved BD and BA privacy budget allocation methods based on sliding windows, we compare the results with the Sample method and the Uniform method. The Sample method randomly selects one publishing time

TABLE 3.3 Comparison of time complexity.

Algorithm	Time complexity
DBP	$O(hn)$
HDPHD	$O(n^2)$
UBQP	$O(hn)$
ATGD	$O(3n)$
GCDPP	$O(2n)$
Proposed Algorithm	$O(2n)$

from w data snapshots and uses the total privacy budget ε to perturb the statistical results at that time. The Uniform method distributes the same budget $\varepsilon_i = \frac{\varepsilon}{w}$ to the statistical results at each publishing time.

Throughout the experiment, all of the privacy budget allocation methods employ the same publishing times, data snapshots sampled from $Data1$ and $Data2$, and partition structures on each data snapshot. Let the total privacy budget $\varepsilon = 0.5$ and use mean absolute error (MAE) and mean relative error (MRE) to measure the deviation between published results and actual statistical values.

$$MAE = \frac{1}{N} \sum_{i=1}^{N} |y_i - \hat{y}_i| \tag{3.19}$$

$$MRE = \frac{1}{N} \sum_{i}^{N} |\frac{y_i - \hat{y}_i}{y_i}| \tag{3.20}$$

Figure 3.18 and Figure 3.19 portray the MAE and MRE of various privacy budget allocation algorithms with different window lengths. It can be observed that the results of the Sample method differ significantly from the other three methods. The improved BD and BA methods have lower MAE and MRE values than other methods.

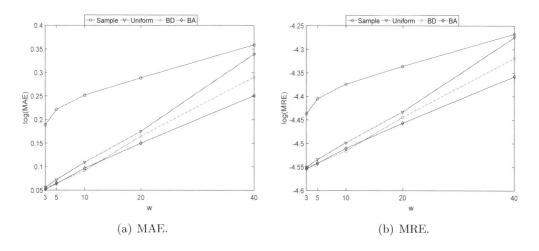

(a) MAE.　　　　　　　　　　　　　　　　(b) MRE.

Figure 3.18 Comparison of privacy budget allocation methods on Data1.

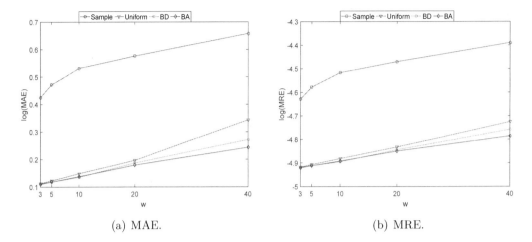

(a) MAE. (b) MRE.

Figure 3.19 Comparison of privacy budget allocation methods on Data2.

With the increase of the size of w, the MAE and MRE of all the privacy budget allocation methods gradually increase. The primary reason is that as the length of windows increases, the privacy budget allocated to each publishing time will gradually decrease, which will increase the noise added at each publishing time. The above experiments prove that compared with typical privacy budget allocation algorithms, the improved BD and BA budget allocation methods perform better on different datasets and different window sizes, which can provide better quality for location-based services.

3.8 CONCLUSION

The widespread popularity of positioning devices and mobile smart terminals has produced a large amount of data with location information. Various location-based big data services have started and represented a new wave of value creation. However, the sensitivity of location information makes the related privacy protection issues extremely urgent. How to provide high-quality location-based services based on protecting users' privacy is the top priority of current research. This chapter focuses on the dynamic statistical publishing and privacy protection of location-based data. An adaptive sampling algorithm based on PID and the data variation difference is proposed to adjust the publishing interval dynamically. A grid clustering and adjustment algorithm is designed based on the high spatial-temporal correlation between adjacent snapshots, which reduces unnecessary calculations in the partitioning process. The dynamic privacy budget allocation method is improved for the continuous publishing process to realize the sliding window-based differential privacy protection of statistical publishing.

However, the study still has some limitations. Firstly, the real-time updating of location data makes the big data publishing related to it should be an uncertain data stream that grows infinitely over time. Therefore, the research of publishing privacy protection based on streaming data is one of our future directions. Secondly, most of the current 2D partition algorithms are based on tree structure or grid structure. However, in real life, most of the areas where people live and work are divided into irregular shapes by roads and other infrastructures, and cannot be well expressed with grid or tree structures. Therefore, the privacy protection dynamic statistical publishing of big data based on road network structure is another research direction in the future.

CHAPTER 4

Localized Location Privacy Protection Based on Optimized Random Response

L OCAL differential privacy model allows users to individually process and protect sensitive personal information, which facilitates avoiding privacy attacks that arise from untrustworthy third-party data collectors. In view of the complex encoding mechanism and low availability of the current location privacy protection methods, a local differential privacy location protection method based on optimized random responses is proposed in this chapter. A spatial decomposition and Hilbert encoding mechanism are designed based on the Hilbert curve, which can reduce the two-dimensional location data into one-dimensional Hilbert encoding results. A local differential privacy location perturbation method based on optimized random response is proposed to improve the availability of perturbed locations and the accuracy of data aggregation. Experiments on actual location datasets prove that the proposed method can provide better location data availability and operational efficiency based on realizing local differential privacy protection of users' locations.

4.1 INTRODUCTION

Traditional location information collection is based on the assumption that the platform performing the location information collection task is authentic and trustworthy. However, in practical applications, even if third-party data collection platforms do not actively steal or leak users' sensitive information, they still cannot effectively guarantee the security of the data they collect and store. Users' real location may still be revealed due to equipment failure, communication hijacking, cyber-attacks, and other problems, triggering a series of reactions. In recent years, there have been numerous data leakage incidents and hacking attacks on various large-scale websites and cloud platforms, which have resulted in record economic losses and adverse impacts.

 DOI: 10.1201/9781003546344-4

To solve these problems, the local differential privacy (LDP) model [142,143] has been proposed, which transfers the privacy processing from the centralized third-party to the user side and eliminates the reliance on third-party servers. Therefore, users can protect their sensitive information according to personal needs. Location collection and privacy protection based on LDP model can provide more effective privacy protection for end-users, which is expected to truly solve the privacy protection problem that restricts the development of location big data.

User-side location privacy protection methods based on the LDP model usually employ a random response mechanism to perturb the location encoding. It is prone to problems such as complex encoding process, high communication cost between the user side and the server side, and low availability of location data after perturbation. To overcome these problems, this chapter proposes a localized location protection method based on optimized random response (LDPORR). The main contributions are as follows:

- A 2D spatial decomposition and Hilbert encoding mechanism is designed based on the partition order of the Hilbert curve, which reduces the two-dimensional location data into one-dimensional Hilbert encoding results.

- A local differential privacy location protection method based on optimized random response is proposed, which improves the availability of perturbed locations and the accuracy of data aggregation.

- Extensive experiments and comparisons are conducted on real location datasets to demonstrate the advantages of the proposed method in terms of the availability of perturbed location, loss of QoS, and the efficiency and overhead of the location privacy protection algorithm.

4.2 STATE OF THE ART

Location privacy protection on the user side can be achieved by randomly generating fake locations or forming location anonymity with other users. Shen *et al.* [111] propose a location privacy-preserving approach based on a locally sensitive hashing algorithm that replaces the GPS coordinates of users' real locations with a set of points of interest around him. Considering that attackers may use auxiliary information such as data analytics and crawlers to determine the approximate location, Liu *et al.* [112] use probability density functions to generate fake location and achieve K-anonymity with privacy region awareness in LBS. Zhang *et al.* [144] combine the idea of irregular polygons to generate polygonal anonymous regions and generate fake locations by setting density parameters. Sun *et al.* [145] propose a location protection method based on point-of-interest segmentation, which generates fake location with the consideration of location semantic and reduces the likelihood of users' real location being exposed. Peng *et al.* [146] suggeste to select $2K$ reasonable fake locations in the anonymized region, and then filter out $K - 1$ locations from them to achieve better anonymity based on the location entropy. In order to improve the effectiveness of the selected fake locations under road network constraints, the method proposed by Xu *et al.* [147] use entropy to denote the degree of anonymity and introduces effective distance to characterize the location distribution. By maximizing the anonymity entropy and effective distance for the set of candidate locations, the uncertainty and dispersion of the selected virtual locations are thus ensured. Although the above-mentioned methods can protect the precise location of the user end from being leaked, they may lead to a serious degradation of the location service quality and increase the query processing overhead of the LBS server. In addition, the security of the above methods is not guaranteed when attackers have obtained some background knowledge about users' locations.

Location privacy protection schemes based on the LDP model implement the protection processing of location data directly on the user side, avoiding the risk of privacy leakage that may be faced after the location submitted to the third-party server. The LDP spatial range query method proposed by Zhang *et al.* [148] indexes the 2D spatial region with a quadtree, and uses a random response mechanism to locally perturb users' locations encoding to achieve user-side location privacy protection. Zhu *et al.* [149] utilize the LDP model to support continuous location sharing between mobile users. Errounda *et al.* [150] propose a sliding window method to address the problem of publishing location statistics with local differential privacy over multiple timestamps. Yan *et al.* [151] combine the Hilbert spacial filling curve to achieve dimension reduction of 2D location data. Random response was implemented on the Hilbert coding result corresponding to users' locations, therefore, the magnitude of the location perturbation is greatly reduced and the availability of the location data is improved. To solve the truck trajectory privacy problem in smart logistics, Yang *et al.* [152] propose a perturbation method using location generalization and local differential privacy. Their solution can preserve the privacy of truck trajectories while maintaining a strong correlation between adjacent spatiotemporal nodes in the trajectory. The location privacy protection method proposed by Hong *et al.* [153] generates perturbed location according to the joint probability distribution function, which has a higher probability density near the original location and a lower probability density in other regions. Wang *et al.* [154] propose a localized differential privacy-preserving framework for LBS scenarios. The proposed staircase randomized response mechanism extends the empirical estimation and significantly improves the utility in different LBS applications. Hong *et al.* [155] addresses the problem of collecting individual locations under local differential privacy by proposing a perturbation mechanism that minimizes the expected error of the perturbed location.

4.3 PRIOR KNOWLEDGE

To facilitate the understanding of subsequent definitions and descriptions, we first provide a unified explanation of the mathematical notations defined and employed in this chapter (as depicted in Table 4.1).

TABLE 4.1   Mathematical notations.

Symbol	Description
ε	Privacy budget
P	Perturbation probability matrix
p_{ij}	Conditional probability from the actual situation i to the response j
f_i	The proportion of element i in the overall data
$Dom(G)$	Spacial domain of 2D planar area G
m	The minimum service scope of LBS
(x_i, y_i)	Original location of user i
N	Partition Granularity
h	Partition order of Hilbert curve
$\mathbb{G}_{N \times N}$	Spacial decomposition results of area G with partition granularity N
$\mathbb{Z}_{N \times N}$	Entire Hilbert encoding of area G with partition granularity N
$\mathbb{I}_{N \times N}$	Distribution density of area G with partition granularity N
Z_i	Original Hilbert encoding of the sub-grid where user i is located
Z_i'	The perturbed Hilbert encoding of user i
b_j	The jth bit of the original Hilbert encoding
b_j'	The jth bit of the perturbed Hilbert encoding
RE	The relative error of range counting query
$Average_{dis}$	Average distance between the real location and the perturbed location

4.3.1   Local Differential Privacy

To avoid the potential disclosure of users' privacy caused by untrustworthy third-party collection platforms, the LDP model quantifies the level of privacy protection while taking into account the knowledge background of attackers. Each user can complete localized differential privacy processing of their data independently and send the processed data to the collection platform. Therefore, users' sensitive information will not be compromised regardless of the trustworthiness of the collection platform, which increased the security of data on the user side.

Definition 4.1 ε-Local differential privacy [142,143]: Let the privacy budget $\varepsilon \in \{\mathbb{R} \geq 0\}$, if an obfuscation algorithm K obtains the same output result y for any two input data x_1, x_2 and satisfies the following inequality, then the obfuscation algorithm K provides ε-local differential privacy.

$$Pr[K(x_1) = y] \leq e^{\varepsilon} \cdot Pr[K(x_2) = y] \tag{4.1}$$

Local differential privacy can be seen as an implementation of differential privacy on individual record. Attackers are unable to infer the specific input data through the output results of the algorithm K, thereby ensuring the security of the data. Wherein, privacy budget ε represents the intensity of privacy protection. A smaller value of ε indicates a higher intensity of privacy protection.

As depicted in Theorem 3.1 and 3.2, the differential privacy model has the serial and parallel combination properties. The former emphasizes that the privacy budget can be allocated at different steps of the random algorithm, while the later ensures that algorithms that satisfy differential privacy are private on disjoint subsets of their datasets. In contrast to the differential privacy model, which is defined on a pair of sibling datasets, the local differential privacy model is defined on two of the records, and the form of the privacy guarantee has not changed. Therefore, the local differential privacy model inherits the above two properties.

Theorem 4.1 *Serial combination property* [136]: For a set of random algorithms $\{K_1, K_2, ..., K_n\}$ working on the same dataset T, wherein K_i $(1 \le i \le n)$ satisfies the ε_i-local differential privacy. Then, the combination of the set of random algorithms, $\{K_1, K_2, ..., K_n\}$, can achieve ε-local differential privacy on the dataset T, wherein $\varepsilon = \sum\limits_{i=1}^{n} \varepsilon_i$.

Theorem 4.2 *Parallel combination property* [136]: Suppose a dataset T can be divided into multiple independent and disjoint subsets, $\{T_1, T_2, ..., T_n\}$. Let K be any random algorithm that satisfies ε-local differential privacy. Then the random algorithm K can achieve ε-local differential privacy on the subsets $\{T_1, T_2, ..., T_n\}$.

4.3.2 Randomized Response Mechanism

The randomized response mechanism proposed by Warner *et al.* [156] is one of the main methods for achieving local differential privacy protection. It has been widely used in the investigation of privacy problems. The main idea of the randomized response mechanism is to utilize the uncertainty of the answers to sensitive binary questions for the privacy protection of the real answers.

Definition 4.2 *Randomized Response [156]: Suppose that every person in a population belongs to either Group A or Group B, and it is required to estimate by survey the proportion belonging to Group A. A random sample of n people is drawn from the population and each person is required to be interviewed. Each interviewer is furnished with an identical spinner which points to the letter A with probability p and to the letter B with probability $(1 - p)$. Each of the interviewee is required to spin the spinner and say 'Yes' or 'No' according to whether or not the spinner points to his correct group. The interviewer needs to statistically analyze the answers received from n interviewees.*

Let n_1 be the number interviewees with answer 'Yes' and π is the true probability of A in the population. $X_i = 1$ if the ith interviewee says 'Yes' while $X_i = 0$ if the ith interviewee says 'No'. Then:

$$P[X_i = 1] = \pi p + (1 - \pi)(1 - p) \tag{4.2}$$

$$P[X_i = 0] = (1 - \pi)p + \pi(1 - p) \tag{4.3}$$

The maximum likelihood estimate of π is:

$$\widehat{\pi} = \frac{p - 1}{2p - 1} + \frac{n_1}{(2p - 1)n} \tag{4.4}$$

which is an unbiased estimate of the true population proportion π.

For a randomized response with only binary answers, the perturbation probability matrix P can be expressed as:

$$P = \begin{pmatrix} p_{00} & p_{01} \\ p_{10} & p_{11} \end{pmatrix} = \begin{pmatrix} p & 1-p \\ 1-p & p \end{pmatrix} \tag{4.5}$$

wherein p_{ij} is the conditional probability from the actual situation i to the response j. This random response mechanism satisfies local differential privacy with a privacy budget $\varepsilon = max\{\ln \frac{p}{1-p}, \ln \frac{1-p}{p}\}$.

4.3.3 Optimized Random Response Mechanism

Randomized response mechanism uses a fixed perturbation probability matrix, which does not ensure that the frequency of the target data is consistent before and after the perturbation. When using such a random response mechanism to achieve localized data privacy protection, the results of data aggregation analysis may significantly differ from the actual situation, seriously destroying the availability of perturbed data. The optimized random response mechanism [157] analyzed the utility problem of the local differential privacy model and designed different perturbation probability matrices according to the initial distribution of data. Under the same level of privacy protection, the optimized random response mechanism can ensure consistent frequency of the target data before and after perturbation, thereby, helping data collectors obtain more accurate data aggregation analysis results.

Still considering the example of a sensitive question survey in Definition 4.2. The randomized response to the sensitive question can be abstracted as the following model: the information of data provider comes from the input alphabet $X = \{0, 1\}$, and the perturbed result belongs to the alphabet $Y = \{0, 1\}$. Let f_i be the proportion of element i ($i \in \{0, 1\}$) in the overall data, there is $0 \leq f_i \leq 1$ and $f_0 + f_1 = 1$. Therefore, the accuracy of data aggregation after using randomized response can be evaluated using the mathematical expectation of the total records with the same input and output.

$$E = f_0 \times p_{00} + f_1 \times p_{11} \tag{4.6}$$

To get the maximum value of the above-mentioned mathematical expectation, the optimized random response mechanism selects the linear programming method with the following constraint conditions:

$$\begin{cases} 1 - p_{11} \leq e^{\varepsilon} p_{00} \\ 1 - p_{00} \leq e^{\varepsilon} p_{11} \\ p_{00} \leq e^{\varepsilon} (1 - p_{11}) \\ p_{11} \leq e^{\varepsilon} (1 - p_{00}) \\ 0 \leq p_{00}, p_{11} \leq 1 \end{cases} \tag{4.7}$$

wherein, for $\forall j \in Y$ and $\forall i_1, i_2 \in X$ there is $p_{i_1 j} \leq e^{\varepsilon} \cdot p_{i_2 j}$ according to the definition of LDP model.

Figure 4.1 depicts the feasible domain of the constraints (4.7), wherein the coordinates of the intersections of the constraints are $A(0, 1)$, $B(\frac{1}{e^{\varepsilon}+1}, \frac{1}{e^{\varepsilon}+1})$, $C(1, 0)$, $D(\frac{e^{\varepsilon}}{e^{\varepsilon}+1}, \frac{e^{\varepsilon}}{e^{\varepsilon}+1})$. The objective function $maximize\{E\}$ has a gradient value of $-\frac{f_0}{f_1}$.

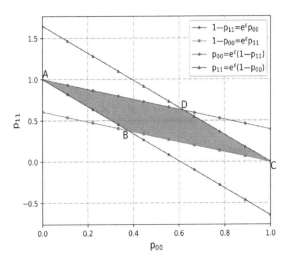

Figure 4.1   Feasible domain of the constraints (4.7) $(\varepsilon = 0.5)$.

4.4   PROPOSED METHOD

The local differential privacy model achieves location privacy protection by perturbing users' original locations or the encoding results of their locations on the use side, so that data collectors and potential attackers will not receive accurate location information from users. However, the inaccuracy caused by location perturbation will destroy the availability of location data, making it impossible for LBS suppliers to provide high-quality service results to users. Subsequent data mining and analysis conducted on the collected perturbed locations will not receive statistical results that are consistent with reality. Therefore, improving the availability of the perturbed location data while ensuring location privacy on the user side is a problem worth studying.

Figure 4.2 portrays the framework of the proposed local differential privacy location protection method based on the optimized random response (LDPORR). Firstly, the server-side partitions the two-dimensional flat area where the city is located into uniformly sized grids based on the accuracy of location-based services. Hilbert encoding is performed on all the corresponding grids and then published to each user. Then, each user can determine the grid area he belongs to by using his real location and the parameters issued by the server. He can obtain the Hilbert encoding results corresponding to his belonging grid area and use the proposed LDPORR mechanism to perturb it. Together with the location-based service request, the user's perturbed location will be submitted to the LBS server instead of his original location. Finally, the server uses the Hilbert decoding algorithm to map the perturbed codes submitted by the user to its corresponding grid region and provides LBS results to the user based on this. By collecting and decoding the perturbed codes from all the users, the server can also realize the statistical analysis of the number of users and regional distribution density within the city based on the initial grid partition structure.

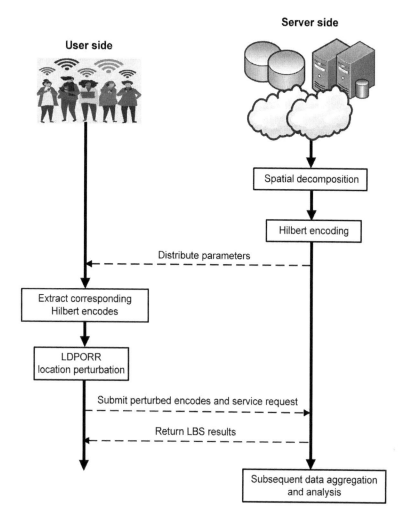

Figure 4.2   Framework of the proposed method.

4.4.1   Spatial Partition and Hilbert Encoding

Grid partitioning is a common method to realize spatial decomposition, which is widely used in traffic volume statistics and LBS applications. To facilitate the random response perturbation of the spatial decomposition results and achieve location privacy protection, the Hilbert encoding method [151] is introduced to map the grid structure into a 0/1 bit sequence.

Figure 4.3 depicts the effect of the first-order Hilbert curve, which separates a two-dimensional area into four equal grids and sorts them into quadrants. The number in each grid is a unique identifier of its grid area. Divide each quadrant of the first-order partition into four sub-grids again and adjust the opening direction of the Hilbert curve, the second-order Hilbert curve can be obtained by connecting all the sub-grids according to the partition order and quadrant. Analogously, higher-order Hilbert curves can be obtained through sub-grids segmentation and curve rotation (Figure 4.4 portrays a third-order Hilbert curve).

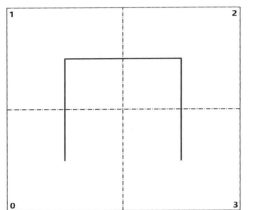

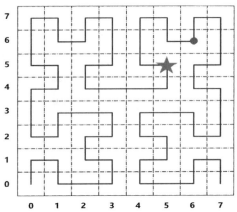

Figure 4.3 The first-order of Hilbert curve. Figure 4.4 The third-order of Hilbert curve.

Definition 4.3 *Partition order of Hilbert curve: For a 2D planar area G with spacial domain Dom(G), it can be partitioned into N × N sub-grids according to Eq. (4.8). The partition order of the Hilbert curve generated on this 2D planar area can be expressed as Eq. (4.9).*

$$N = \sqrt{Dom(G)/m} \qquad (4.8)$$

$$h = \lceil \log_2 N \rceil \qquad (4.9)$$

wherein m represents the minimum service scope of LBS. The higher the accuracy of location-based service provided by the server, the smaller the value of m, the more sub-grids obtained through spatial partitioning, and the higher the order of the Hilbert curve.

Each order of the Hilbert curve separates the current region into four sub-regions of the same size. Therefore, only two binary bits are needed to encode the generated sub-regions. The Hilbert encoding results of adjacent sub-regions also have similarity, which maintains good spatial clustering characteristics. Algorithm 4.1 depicts the Hilbert encoding process on the server side. The 2D planar area of the city is firstly partitioned into equal-sized sub-grids according to Eq. (4.8) and the order of the Hilbert curve is determined according to Eq. (4.9). Lines 4-25 obtain the Hilbert encoding of each sub-grid. Line 26 returns the overall Hilbert encoding results of the 2D planar area. Subsequently, the LBS server will distribute the spacial decomposition results $\mathbb{G}_{N \times N}$ together with the integral Hilbert encoding $\mathbb{Z}_{N \times N}$ to all the users.

Time-complexity of Algorithm 4.1: For a 2D planar area with partition granularity N, the sever side first spend $O(N)$ time complexity to implement grid partition (lines 1∼2). Then, it needs $O(N \log N)$ time complexity to carry out the Hilbert encoding process for each sub-grid region (lines 4∼25). Therefore, the overall time complexity of Algorithm 4.1 is $O(N + N \log N) \approx O(N \log N)$.

Take the third-order Hilbert curve depicted in Figure 4.5 for example. One user (represented by the red point) is located in the sub-grid with coordinate pair (6,6).

Algorithm 4.1 Hilbert encoding algorithm (on the server side).

Input: Spacial domain of the 2D planar area $Dom(G)$; the minimum service scope of LBS m

Output: The integral Hilbert encoding results $\mathbb{Z}_{N \times N}$

1: The server determines the partition granularity N and the partition order of Hilbert curve h according to formulas (5) and (6)
2: Partition the 2D planar area into $N \ddot{O} N$ equal sized sub-grids according to partition granularity N
3: Initialize the integral Hilbert encoding $\mathbb{Z}_{N \times N} = \{\}$
4: **for** each sub-grid with coordinate pair (i, j) **do**
5:    $U_{i,j} = \{\}$
6:    $w = 2^{h-1}$
7:    $t = 1$
8:    **for** $h \neq 0$ **do**
9:       Determine the belonging quadrant for sub-grid (i, j) on the tth order of Hilbert curve
10:       $U_{i,j} \longleftarrow$ obtain the quadrant number Q
11:       **if** $Q = 0$ **then**
12:          $(i, j) = (j, i)$
13:       **else if** $Q = 1$ **then**
14:          $(i, j) = (i, j - w)$
15:       **else if** $Q = 2$ **then**
16:          $(i, j) = (i - w, j - w)$
17:       **else if** $Q = 3$ **then**
18:          $(i, j) = (w - j - 1, w \times 2 - i - 1)$
19:       **end if**
20:       $h = h - 1$
21:       $w = w/2$
22:       $t = t + 1$
23:    **end for**
24:    $\mathbb{Z}_{N \times N} \longleftarrow$ convert each bit in $U_{i,j}$ to binary
25: **end for**
26: return $\mathbb{Z}_{N \times N}$

In the first-order of Hilbert curve partition results, the sub-grid where the user is located belongs to quadrant 2. Therefore, we receive the encoding result $\{10\}$ for the first-order partition. Then, in the second order of the sub-grid partition, the user belongs to quadrant 2. Therefore, the encoding result for the second-order partition will also be $\{10\}$. In the third order of the sub-grid partition, the user locates in quadrant 0, so the encoding result will be $\{00\}$. The final Hilbert encoding results of the sub-grid where the user is located will be $\{101000\}$.

4.4.2 Localized Perturbation Mechanism Based on Optimized Random Response

To realize location privacy protection on the user side, the Hilbert encoding result of the grid where the user is located can be randomly perturbed and submitted to the LBS server instead of his original location. However, traditional randomized response mechanisms may randomly perturb any bit of the Hilbert encoding result, leaving no statistical correlations between the output encoding string and the input encoding string. The location corresponding to the perturbed result may be far from the user's original location. Although the goal of location privacy protection has been achieved, it is difficult to obtain satisfactory LBS service results based on such a perturbed location, which seriously damages the service quality of LBS applications. Subsequent data analysis and mining results based on such perturbed locations are less likely to obtain useful information.

Since the result of Hilbert encoding is a binary composed of 0 and 1, and the Hilbert encoding results of adjacent grids also have similarity, therefore, the perturbation result will have good usability only when the frequency of 0 and 1 in the output encoding string is consistent with that of the input encoding string. Based on the above analysis, this section designs a perturbation method for Hilbert encoding results based on the optimized random response mechanism.

Let $P = \begin{pmatrix} p_{00} & p_{01} \\ p_{10} & p_{11} \end{pmatrix}$ be the perturbation matrix, wherein p_{ij} is the conditional probability from the actual situation i to the response j, $0 \leq p_{ij} \leq 1$, $p_{00} + p_{01} = 1$, and $p_{10} + p_{11} = 1$. Use f_0 and f_1 to represent the proportion of elements 0 and 1 in the input encoding string. Combining the optimized random response feasible region shown in Figure 4.2, the following scenarios can be obtained:

(1) When $\frac{f_0}{f_1} \leq e^{-\varepsilon}$, the mathematical expectation (depicted in eq. (4.6)) of the total records with the same input and output reaches the optimal solution at point A, wherein the conditional probabilities are $p_{00} = 0$ and $p_{11} = 1$. Therefore, the optimal value of the mathematical expectation is $E = f_1$. To achieve the best accuracy of data aggregation after using random response, the perturbation matrix can be designed as $P = \begin{pmatrix} 0 & 1 \\ 0 & 1 \end{pmatrix}$.

(2) When $e^{-\varepsilon} < \frac{f_0}{f_1} < e^{\varepsilon}$, the mathematical expectation reaches the optimal solution at point D, and the optimal value of the mathematical expectation is $\frac{e^{\varepsilon}}{e^{\varepsilon}+1}$. To achieve the best accuracy of data aggregation, the perturbation matrix of the random response mechanism can be designed as $P = \begin{pmatrix} \frac{e^{\varepsilon}}{e^{\varepsilon}+1} & \frac{1}{e^{\varepsilon}+1} \\ \frac{1}{e^{\varepsilon}+1} & \frac{e^{\varepsilon}}{e^{\varepsilon}+1} \end{pmatrix}$.

(3) When $\frac{f_0}{f_1} \geq e^{\varepsilon}$, the mathematical expectation reaches the optimal solution at point C, wherein the conditional probabilities are $p_{00} = 1$ and $p_{11} = 0$. Therefore, the optimal value of the mathematical expectation is $E = f_0$. To achieve the best accuracy of data aggregation, the random response perturbation matrix can be designed as $P = \begin{pmatrix} 1 & 0 \\ 1 & 0 \end{pmatrix}$.

Based on the above analysis, the optimized random response for Hilbert encoding results is proposed to select different perturbation matrices according to the frequency ratio of 0 and 1 in the input Hilbert encoding and maintain consistent distribution before and after perturbation.

Definition 4.4 *Optimized random response for Hilbert encoding: Let b_j and b'_j be the jth bit of the original and perturbed Hilbert encoding respectively, f_0 and f_1 represent the proportion of element 0 and 1 in the Hilbert encoding. The optimized random response for Hilbert encoding can be obtained by perturbing each bit of the encoding string according to the following probability equations (4.10):*

$$\Pr\left[b'_j = b_j\right] = \begin{cases} \begin{array}{ll} 1, & b_j = 1 \\ & \\ 0, & b_j = 0 \end{array}, & if \quad \frac{f_0}{f_1} \le e^{-\varepsilon} \\ \\ \begin{array}{ll} \frac{e^\varepsilon}{1+e^\varepsilon}, b_j = 1 \quad or \quad 0 \\ & \\ \frac{1}{1+e^\varepsilon}, b_j = 0 \quad or \quad 1 \end{array}, & if \quad e^{-\varepsilon} < \frac{f_0}{f_1} < e^\varepsilon \\ \\ \begin{array}{ll} 1, & b_j = 0 \\ & \\ 0, & b_j = 1 \end{array}, & if \quad \frac{f_0}{f_1} \ge e^\varepsilon \end{cases} \quad (4.10)$$

Algorithm 4.2 portrays the process of the optimized random response for Hilbert encoding on the user side. A mobile user can firstly determine his belonging sub-grid with his original location (x_i, y_i) and the spacial decomposition results $\mathbb{G}_{N \times N}$ delivered by the server. Then, the user can extract the corresponding Hilbert code Z_i for his belonging sub-grid from the integral Hilbert encoding results $\mathbb{Z}_{N \times N}$ distributed by the server. Finally, the optimized random response was implemented on each bit of the Hilbert encoding according to Eq. (4.10). Lines 12~25 of Algorithm 4.2 ensure that in some extreme cases of Hilbert encoding, for example, {000000} and {111111}, the optimized random response still retains the original encoding information, keeping highly similarity of the Hilbert encoding results before and after perturbation. Therefore, the user's location is perturbed by a neighbouring grid or remains untouched, and the availability of the perturbed location has been improved.

Time-complexity of Algorithm 4.2: For a 2D planar area with partition granularity N, the user side first spends $O(\log N)$ time complexity to traverse the Hilbert encoding results representing his location (lines 4~11) and obtain the distribution frequencies of 0 and 1. Then, the user side needs $O(\log N)$ time complexity to select a suitable perturbation scheme and carry out the perturbation on each bit of the original Hilbert encoding results (lines 12~25). Therefore, the overall time complexity of Algorithm 4.2 is $O(\log N + \log N) \approx O(\log N)$.

Corollary 1: The proposed local differential privacy location protection algorithm based on optimized random response (LDPORR), can provide ε-local differential privacy protection for mobile users.

Algorithm 4.2 Local differential privacy location protection algorithm based on optimized random response (on the user side)

Input: Spacial decomposition results $\mathbb{G}_{N \times N}$, the integral Hilbert encoding $\mathbb{Z}_{N \times N}$, user's original location (x_i, y_i), privacy budget ε.

Output: User's perturbation Hilbert encoding Z'_i.

1: User determines his belonging sub-grid with his original location (x_i, y_i) and the spacial decomposition results $\mathbb{G}_{N \times N}$ delivered by the server

2: Extract the original Hilbert encoding Z_i from $\mathbb{Z}_{N \times N}$ according to user's belonging sub-grid

3: $c_0 = 0, c_1 = 0$

4: **for** each bit $b_{j(1 \leq j \leq 2 \log_2 N)}$ in Z_i **do**

5:     **if** $b_j = 0$ **then**

6:         $c_0 = c_0 + 1$

7:     **else**

8:         $c_1 = c_1 + 1$

9:     **end if**

10: **end for**

11: $f_0 = \frac{c_0}{c_0 + c_1}, f_1 = \frac{c_1}{c_0 + c_1}$

12: **if** $e^{-\varepsilon} < \frac{f_0}{f_1} < e^{\varepsilon}$ **then**

13:     **for** each bit b_j in Z_i **do**

14:         $\Pr\left[Z'_i\left(b'_j\right) = b_j \mid Z_i\left(b_j\right)\right] = \frac{e^{\varepsilon}}{1 + e^{\varepsilon}}$

15:         $\Pr\left[Z'_i\left(b'_j\right) \neq b_j \mid Z_i\left(b_j\right)\right] = \frac{1}{1 + e^{\varepsilon}}$

16:     **end for**

17: **else if** $\frac{f_0}{f_1} \geq e^{\varepsilon}$ **then**

18:     **for** each bit b_j in Z_i **do**

19:         $\Pr\left[Z'_i\left(b'_j\right) = 0 \mid Z_i\left(b_j\right)\right] = 1$

20:     **end for**

21: **else if** $\frac{f_0}{f_1} \leq e^{-\varepsilon}$ **then**

22:     **for** each bit b_j in Z_i **do**

23:         $\Pr\left[Z'_i\left(b'_j\right) = 1 \mid Z_i\left(b_j\right)\right] = 1$

24:     **end for**

25: **end if**

26: return Z'_i

Proof: Let Z_i and Z'_i be the original and perturbed Hilbert encoding of user i respectively, b_j and b'_j are the jth bit of the original and perturbed Hilbert encoding. The length of the Hilbert encoding is $2h$, wherein h is the partition order of the Hilbert curve. Combined with the parallel combination property of the local differential privacy model, there is:

$$\Pr\left[Z'_i \mid Z_i\right] = \prod_{j=1}^{2h} \Pr\left[Z'_i(b'_j) \mid Z_i(b_j)\right]$$

Similarly, for another probable Hilbert encoding Z^*_i of user i, there is:

$$\Pr\left[Z'_i \mid Z^*_i\right] = \prod_{j=1}^{2h} \Pr\left[Z'_i(b'_j) \mid Z^*_i(b_j)\right]$$

According to the proposed local differential privacy location protection algorithm based on optimized random response (LDPORR), we can discuss the following scenarios:

(1) When $\frac{f_0}{f_1} \leq e^{-\varepsilon}$, the proposed LDPORR algorithm adopts the perturbation matrix $P = \begin{pmatrix} 0 & 1 \\ 0 & 1 \end{pmatrix}$. Then, here is:

$$\frac{\Pr\left[Z_i' \mid Z_i\right]}{\Pr\left[Z_i' \mid Z_i^*\right]} = \frac{\Pr\left[Z_i'(b_1') = 1, \ldots, Z_i'(b_{2h}') = 1 \mid Z_i\right]}{\Pr\left[Z_i'(b_1') = 1, \ldots, Z_i'(b_{2h}') = 1 \mid Z_i^*\right]}$$

$$= \frac{\prod\limits_{j=1}^{2h} \Pr\left[Z_i'(b_j') = 1 \mid Z_i(b_j)\right]}{\prod\limits_{j=1}^{2h} \Pr\left[Z_i'(b_j') = 1 \mid Z_i^*(b_j)\right]}$$

$$= \frac{\Pr\left[Z_i'(b_j') = 1 \mid Z_i(b_j)\right]}{\Pr\left[Z_i'(b_j') = 1 \mid Z_i^*(b_j)\right]}$$

$$= 1 \leq e^{\varepsilon}$$

(2) When $e^{-\varepsilon} < \frac{f_0}{f_1} < e^{\varepsilon}$, the perturbation matrix $P = \begin{pmatrix} \frac{e^{\varepsilon}}{e^{\varepsilon}+1} & \frac{1}{e^{\varepsilon}+1} \\ \frac{1}{e^{\varepsilon}+1} & \frac{e^{\varepsilon}}{e^{\varepsilon}+1} \end{pmatrix}$ is utilized. Therefore, here is:

$$\frac{\Pr\left[Z_i' \mid Z_i\right]}{\Pr\left[Z_i' \mid Z_i^*\right]} = \frac{\prod\limits_{j=1}^{2h} \Pr\left[Z_i'(b_j') \mid Z_i(b_j)\right]}{\prod\limits_{j=1}^{2h} \Pr\left[Z_i'(b_j') \mid Z_i^*(b_j)\right]}$$

$$= \frac{\Pr\left[Z_i'(b_j') \mid Z_i(b_j)\right]}{\Pr\left[Z_i'(b_j') \mid Z_i^*(b_j)\right]}$$

$$\leq \frac{\max \Pr\left[Z_i'(b_j') \mid Z_i(b_j)\right]}{\min \Pr\left[Z_i'(b_j') \mid Z_i^*(b_j)\right]}$$

$$= \frac{\frac{e^{\varepsilon}}{e^{\varepsilon}+1}}{\frac{1}{e^{\varepsilon}+1}} = e^{\varepsilon}.$$

(3) When $\frac{f_0}{f_1} \geq e^{\varepsilon}$, the perturbation matrix will be $P = \begin{pmatrix} 1 & 0 \\ 1 & 0 \end{pmatrix}$. Then, we have:

$$\frac{\Pr\left[Z_i' \mid Z_i\right]}{\Pr\left[Z_i' \mid Z_i^*\right]} = \frac{\Pr\left[Z_i'(b_1') = 0, \ldots, Z_i'(b_{2h}') = 0 \mid Z_i\right]}{\Pr\left[Z_i'(b_1') = 0, \ldots, Z_i'(b_{2h}') = 0 \mid Z_i^*\right]}$$

$$= \frac{\prod\limits_{j=1}^{2h} \Pr\left[Z_i'(b_j') = 0 \mid Z_i(b_j)\right]}{\prod\limits_{j=1}^{2h} \Pr\left[Z_i'(b_j') = 0 \mid Z_i^*(b_j)\right]}$$

$$= \frac{\Pr\left[Z_i'(b_j') = 0 \mid Z_i(b_j)\right]}{\Pr\left[Z_i'(b_j') = 0 \mid Z_i^*(b_j)\right]}$$

$$= 1 \leq e^{\varepsilon}$$

Combining all the above situations, we can conclude that the proposed LDPORR algorithm can provide ε-local differential privacy protection for the user's location in any circumstances.

4.4.3 Hilbert Decoding and Data Aggregation

After collecting the Hilbert encoding perturbation results of a large number of users, the server side first restores the perturbed Hilbert encoding results to a serial number of a certain grid using the Hilbert decoding algorithm (depicts in Algorithm 4.3), and then, conducts statistical analysis about the number of users on each sub-grid according to the initial grid partition structure.

Let's take the third-order Hilbert curve shown in Figure 4.4 as an illustration. Suppose the proposed LDPORR algorithm perturbs a user's Hilbert encoding from {101000} (represented by the red point) to {100010} (represented by the orange pentagram). The proposed Hilbert decoding algorithm will extract the first two bits of the encoding (i.e., {10}) to determine the location of the user on the first-order Hilbert partition. In this example, the result is that the user locates in quadrant 2 after the first-order Hilbert curve partition, corresponding to the rectangular area within [4,7] both on the horizontal and vertical coordinates. Then, the subsequent two bits {00} were selected to determine the location of the user on the second-order Hilbert partition. Here we have the result that the user locates in quadrant 0, which corresponded to the rectangular area within [4,5] both on the horizontal and vertical coordinates. Finally, the last two bits {10} will be used to determine that the user locates in quadrant 2 of the third-order Hilbert curve partition and the corresponding sub-grid with coordinate pair (5,5).

Time-complexity of Algorithm 4.3: For a 2D planar area with partition granularity N, the server side receives the perturbed Hilbert encoding results from n users and decodes them to get the statistical analysis (lines 2∼31). Therefore, the overall time complexity of Algorithm 4.3 is $O(n \log N)$.

Corollary 2: By utilizing the proposed Hilbert decoding and statistical analysis algorithm depicted in Algorithm 4.3, the server side can obtain the unbiased estimates of users' distribution density.

Proof: The proposed Algorithm 4.3 calculates the number of users in each sub-grid after Hilbert decoding to estimate the distribution density of users, which implies that the distributions of element 0 and 1 in the perturbed encoding have no bias compared with the distribution of the original encoding.

According to Algorithm 4.1, each user will generate a Hilbert encoding with a length of $2h$ bits to represent the sub-grid where he or she is located. Let f_i and f_i' be the proportions of element i in the original and perturbed Hilbert encoding, respectively. There is $i \in \{0, 1\}$, and $0 \leq f_i, f_i' \leq 1$. Let p be the probability of not perturbing each bit of the original Hilbert encoding, and $1 - p$ be the probability of perturbing the bits. Then, the frequencies of elements 0 and 1 in the perturbed Hilbert encoding can be represented as follows:

$$f_0' = f_0 p + (1 - f_0)(1 - p) \tag{4.11}$$

Algorithm 4.3 Hilbert decoding and statistical analysis (on the server side).

Input: Perturbed Hilbert encoding of large number of users $Z' = \{Z_1', Z_2', ..., Z_n'\}$

Output: Users' distribution density $\mathbb{I}_{N \times N}$

1: Initialize $\mathbb{I}_{N \times N} = \{\}$
2: **for** each $Z_k'(1 \le k \le n)$ **do**
3:     $Z_k^* \longleftarrow$ convert each two bits of Z_k' into a quaternion value
4:     $Q' \longleftarrow$ select the last digit of Z_k^*
5:     **if** $Q' = 0$ **then**
6:         $(i', j')=(0, 0)$
7:     **else if** $Q' = 1$ **then**
8:         $(i', j')=(0, 1)$
9:     **else if** $Q' = 2$ **then**
10:         $(i', j')=(1, 1)$
11:     **else if** $Q' = 3$ **then**
12:         $(i', j')=(1, 0)$
13:     **end if**
14:     $v = 2$
15:     **for** $Z_k^* \ne \varnothing$ **do**
16:         $Q' \longleftarrow$ select the last digit of Z_k^*
17:         **if** $Q' = 0$ **then**
18:             $(i', j')=(j', i')$
19:         **else if** $Q' = 1$ **then**
20:             $(i', j')=(i', j' + v)$
21:         **else if** $Q' = 2$ **then**
22:             $(i', j')=(i' + v, j' + v)$
23:         **else if** $Q' = 3$ **then**
24:             $(i', j')=(2v - j' - 1, v - i' - 1)$
25:         **end if**
26:         Delete the last digit of Z_k^*
27:         $v = v \times 2$
28:     **end for**
29:     $\mathbb{I}_{N \times N} \longleftarrow$ increase the number of users in the sub-grid (i', j') by 1
30:     Delete the last digit of Z_k^*
31: **end for**
32: return $\mathbb{I}_{N \times N}$

$$f_1' = (1 - f_0)p + f_0(1 - p) \tag{4.12}$$

To verify that f_i' is an unbiased estimation of f_i, the following likelihood function can be constructed:

$$L = [f_0 p + (1 - f_0)(1 - p)]^{2h \cdot f_0'}[(1 - f_0)p + f_0(1 - p)]^{2h \cdot (1 - f_0')}$$

The following maximum likelihood estimates can be obtained:

$$\widehat{f_0} = \frac{p - 1 + f_0'}{2p - 1} \tag{4.13}$$

$$\widehat{f_1} = 1 - \widehat{f_0} = \frac{p - 1 + f_1'}{2p - 1} \tag{4.14}$$

Calculating the expectations of the maximum likelihood estimation values mentioned above, there is:

$$\begin{aligned} E(\widehat{f_0}) &= \frac{p - 1 + E(f_0')}{2p - 1} \\ &= \frac{p - 1 + f_0 p + (1 - f_0)(1 - p)}{2p - 1} = f_0 \end{aligned}$$

$$\begin{aligned} E(\widehat{f_1}) &= \frac{p - 1 + E(f_1')}{2p - 1} \\ &= \frac{p - 1 + (1 - f_0)p + f_0(1 - p)}{2p - 1} \\ &= 1 - f_0 = f_1 \end{aligned}$$

Therefore, we have proved that $\widehat{f_i}$ is an unbiased estimate of f_i.

Combining the specific perturbation mechanisms adopted in the proposed LD-PORR algorithm, we can discuss the following scenarios:

(1) When $\frac{f_0}{f_1} \leq e^{-\varepsilon}$, the proportion of element 0 in the original Hilbert encoding is very small. There is $\lim f_0 \to 0$. The proposed LDPORR algorithm utilizes the perturbation matrix $P = \begin{pmatrix} 0 & 1 \\ 0 & 1 \end{pmatrix}$. Therefore, the probability of not perturbing is $p = p_{11} = 1$. Substituting this result into Eq. (4.11) and Eq. (4.13), there is:

$$\widehat{f_0} = f_0' = 0$$

Similarly, substituting this result into formulas Eq. (4.12) and Eq. (4.14), there is:

$$\widehat{f_1} = f_1' = 1$$

(2) When $e^{-\varepsilon} < \frac{f_0}{f_1} < e^{\varepsilon}$, the proportions of element 0 and 1 in the original Hilbert encoding is similar. There is $\lim f_0 \to \frac{1}{2}$ and $\lim f_1 \to \frac{1}{2}$. The proposed LDPORR algorithm adopts the perturbation matrix $P = \begin{pmatrix} \frac{e^{\varepsilon}}{e^{\varepsilon}+1} & \frac{1}{e^{\varepsilon}+1} \\ \frac{1}{e^{\varepsilon}+1} & \frac{e^{\varepsilon}}{e^{\varepsilon}+1} \end{pmatrix}$. Therefor, the probability of not perturbing is $p = p_{00} = p_{11} = \frac{e^{\varepsilon}}{e^{\varepsilon}+1}$. Substituting this result into Eq. (4.11) and Eq. (4.13), there is:

$$\widehat{f_0} = f_0' = \frac{1}{2}$$

TABLE 4.2   Properties of experimental datasets.

Datasets	Location range	Volume
$Yellow\_tripdata$	$[40.54°\text{N} \sim 41.02°\text{N}, -74.30°\text{W} \sim -73.52°\text{W}]$	29991
$Tokyo$	$[35.50°\text{N} \sim 35.87°\text{N}, 139.47°\text{E} \sim 139.91°\text{E}]$	573703
$Landmark$	$[24.55°\text{N} \sim 49.00°\text{N} \quad -124.44°\text{W} \sim -67.02°\text{W}]$	870000

Similarly, substituting this result into Eq. (4.12) and Eq. (4.14), there is:

$$\widehat{f_1} = f_1' = \frac{1}{2}$$

(3) When $\frac{f_0}{f_1} \geq e^\varepsilon$, the proportion of element 0 in the original Hilbert encoding is very large. There is $\lim f_0 \to 1$. The proposed LDPORR algorithm utilizes the perturbation matrix $P = \begin{pmatrix} 1 & 0 \\ 1 & 0 \end{pmatrix}$. Therefor, the probability of not perturbing is $p = p_{00} = 1$. Substituting this result into Eq. (4.11) and Eq. (4.13), there is:

$$\widehat{f_0} = f_0' = 1$$

Similarly, substituting this result into Eq. (4.12) and Eq. (4.14), there is:

$$\widehat{f_1} = f_1' = 0$$

To sum up, using the proposed Algorithm 4.3 on the server side to estimate the distribution density of mobile users can obtain unbiased results of the real distribution density of users.

4.5   SIMULATION RESULTS AND PERFORMANCE ANALYSIS

In order to evaluate and analyze the comprehensive performance of the proposed location privacy protection method LDPORR, we compare it with some existing LDP-based location protection methods in terms of range counting query accuracy, location data aggregation accuracy, loss of QoS, and the efficiency and overhead of perturbation algorithm. For the sake of fairness, the comparison algorithms are all based on spatial decomposition and local differential privacy random response. The baseline methods include but are not limited to, the GT-R algorithm [148], the LDPHE algorithm [151], the DPL-Hc algorithm [158], and the LDPart algorithm [159]. Experimental datasets include $Landmark$ [160], which is a location information dataset of 48 states in the United States provided by Infochimps; $Yellow\_tripdata$ [141], a Taxi record dataset provided by the New York City Taxi Management Committee; and $Tokyo$ [161], an LBSNs check-in dataset from Tokyo, Japan. Table 4.2 depicts the specific details of the experimental datasets.

4.5.1   Accuracy of Range Counting Query on Perturbed Locations

Range counting queries are widely used in LBS services to obtain the number of users, vehicles, or facilities within a certain range. We use the accuracy of the range counting query to evaluate the availability of perturbed location data submitted by users. The relative error (RE) of the range counting query indicates the accuracy of LBS services based on the perturbed location data submitted by users. A smaller RE value means that the range-counting query is closer to the real distribution of users. The calculation formula of the relative error is the same as Eq. (3.18) in Chapter 3. The value range of privacy budget ε is set to be [0.4, 2]. The query range covers 40%, 50%, and 60% of the 2D planar area corresponding to the location dataset, respectively. Each of the queries was randomly selected and executed 500 times to determine the average value of relative error. Experimental results are depicted in Figures 4.5, 4.6, and 4.7.

As can be observed from Figures 4.5, 4.6, and 4.7, the relative error of the same algorithm on the same dataset decreases as the privacy budget increases, i.e., the availability of the data increases. The primary reason is that in the local differential privacy model, the privacy budget is the main measurement of the degree of privacy protection. The larger the privacy budget, the less perturbation will be incorporated into the data. Therefore, the relative error before and after perturbation is reduced.

On the same experimental dataset, as the query range increases from small to large, the relative errors of various algorithms also decrease to varying degrees. The reason is that when the query range is small, some users whose real locations are within the query range deviate from the current range after perturbation, resulting in a relatively high error in range counting queries. With the increase in query range, the situation where the user's perturbed location is out of the query range will be decreased. Therefore, the relative error of range counting queries will be reduced.

Compare the relative errors of various perturbation algorithms in the same dataset and query range: the proposed LDPORR algorithm is significantly better than the LDPart and GT-R algorithms, and in most cases better than the LDPHE and DPL-Hc algorithms. The main reason is that, when the dataset is partitioned and encoded with the same granularity, the LDPart algorithm uses a traditional random response method to perturb each bit of the grid encoding, which does not guarantee the similarity before and after perturbation. Therefore, the situation might happen that the corresponding grid after location perturbation is far from the original grid. The GT-R algorithm uses a quadtree structure to partition the 2D planar area and randomly selects a layer of nodes in the quadtree for unary encoding and random response perturbation. However, the perturbation mechanism of the GT-R algorithm is essentially a traditional random response, where the user can randomly select one layer to carry out the perturbation. The high degree of randomness leads to large relative errors. The relative errors of the LDPORR algorithm, LDPHE algorithm, and DPL-Hc algorithm are all smaller than other algorithms. However, the advantage of the LDPORR algorithm is more pronounced as the privacy budget increases, because the LDPORR algorithm applies different perturbation mechanisms to different types of encoding and guarantees the similarity of each type of code before and after the

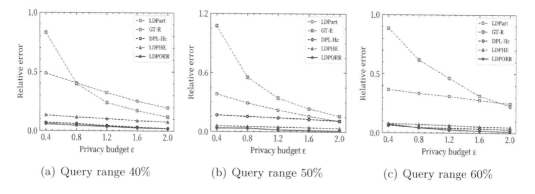

Figure 4.5 Relative error of range counting query on *Yellow_tripdata* dataset.

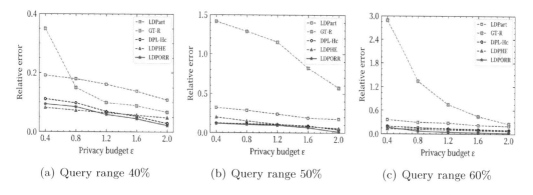

Figure 4.6 Relative error of range counting query on *Tokyo* dataset.

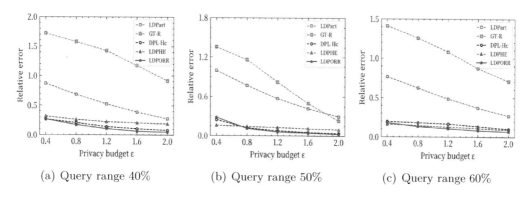

Figure 4.7 Relative error of range counting query on *Landmark* dataset.

perturbation with maximum probability. Combined with the spatial clustering property of Hilbert encoding, the proposed LDPORR algorithm achieves better accuracy of range counting queries than other baseline methods.

4.5.2   Aggregation Accuracy of Perturbed Locations on Server Side

Density statistics is an important way to obtain and analyze the distribution of population, vehicles, facilities, etc. in an area. To verify that the proposed LDPORR algorithm can guarantee the accuracy of location statistical analysis on the server side, density statistical analysis has been implemented on the collected perturbation locations according to the spatial partition granularity. The density statistical results of all the algorithms are compared with the actual results. Since the setting of the privacy budget does not affect the density statistical results before and after perturbation, we only take $\varepsilon = 1.2$ as an example for analysis.

Figures 4.8, 4.9, and 4.10 depict the density statistical results of all the algorithms on different datasets. It is obvious that the LDPart and GT-R algorithms have largely lost the density distribution characteristics of the original dataset. While the LDPORR, LDPHE, and DPL-Hc algorithms better reflect the original density distribution characteristics, with the perturbation results of the LDPORR algorithm being much closer to the original distribution.

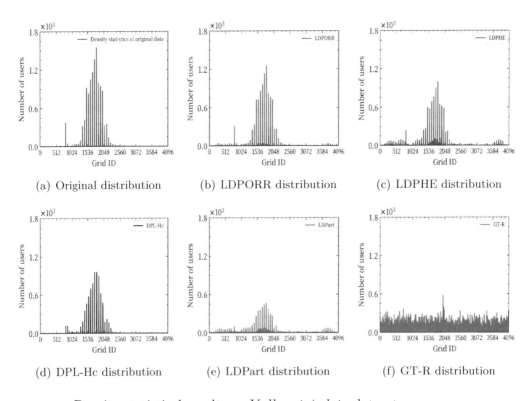

(a) Original distribution   (b) LDPORR distribution   (c) LDPHE distribution

(d) DPL-Hc distribution   (e) LDPart distribution   (f) GT-R distribution

Figure 4.8 Density statistical results on *Yellow_tripdata* dataset.

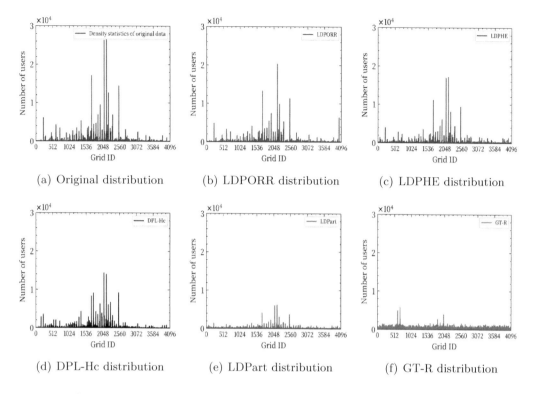

(a) Original distribution   (b) LDPORR distribution   (c) LDPHE distribution

(d) DPL-Hc distribution   (e) LDPart distribution   (f) GT-R distribution

Figure 4.9 Density statistical results on *Tokoy* dataset.

The LDPart and GT-R algorithm utilizes the traditional random response mechanism to perturb each bit of the encoding results, which may perturb the user's location into any of the sub-grid in the global scope. Therefore, the original density distribution characteristics can not be maintained after perturbation. The LDPHE algorithm perturbs only one bit of the encoding, the overall disturbance is not significant compared with the LDPart and GT-R algorithms. Besides, users within adjacent sub-grids may be disturbed into adjacent sub-grids while using the LDPHE algorithm, and the random responses of a large number of users will balance the bias in the statistical results, resulting in better results. The DPL-Hc algorithm adds Laplacian noise to the serial number of sub-grids. Therefore, the disturbed location range is limited within the adjacent sub-grids, to avoid excessive loss of the original density distribution characteristics. The proposed LDPORR algorithm combines the spatial clustering characteristic of the Hilbert curve with the optimized random responses so that the perturbation range of the user's location is compressed with greater probability within the neighboured sub-grids. In addition, the optimized random response incorporates the utilized distribution ratio of bits 0 and 1 in the original encoding to select a suitable perturbation matrix for different situations, which can handle some extreme cases of encoding. Therefore, the proposed LDPORR algorithm achieves better results in terms of density distribution statistics on the server side, providing better quality for subsequent data mining, analysis, and publishing of location big data.

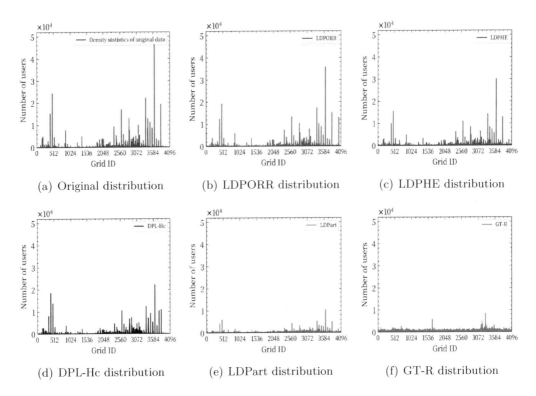

(a) Original distribution   (b) LDPORR distribution   (c) LDPHE distribution

(d) DPL-Hc distribution   (e) LDPart distribution   (f) GT-R distribution

Figure 4.10   Density statistical results on *Landmark* dataset.

4.5.3   Loss of QoS

In order to achieve location privacy protection, a perturbation mechanism has been introduced to perturb the user's location or the encoding results of the user's location. The consequent result brings in some changes in the user's location or the encoding results of the user's location, resulting in a certain loss of service quality in practical LBS applications. In this section, the average distance between the perturbed location and the real location is used to intuitively reflect the quality loss of location-based services caused by different perturbation mechanisms. The definition is depicted in the following Eq. (4.15):

$$Average_{\text{dis}} = \frac{1}{M} \times \sum_{i=1}^{M} \text{dis}\left(x_i, x_i'\right) \tag{4.15}$$

wherein M is the amount of users, x_i and x_i' denote the original and perturbed locations of the i-th user, and $dis(\cdot)$ represents the distance between these two locations.

Figure 4.11 portrays the comparison results of average perturbation distances on different datasets. Each of the algorithms is executed 500 times to determine the average perturbation distances. For the sake of fairness, all the perturbation algorithms use the same spatial decomposition granularity. It is easy to be observed that the average perturbation distance of various algorithms gradually decreases with the increase of privacy budget ε. The primary reason is that the smaller the value of the privacy budget, the greater the perturbation introduced by local differential

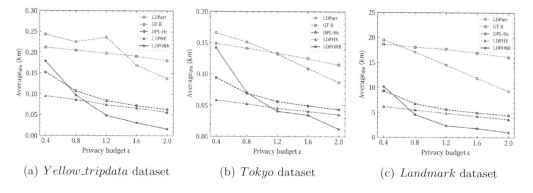

(a) *Yellow_tripdata* dataset   (b) *Tokyo* dataset   (c) *Landmark* dataset

Figure 4.11 Average perturbation distances on different datasets

privacy protection, and the higher the intensity of privacy protection provided. When the privacy budget is the same, the average perturbation distance of the LDPart and the GT-R algorithm is significantly greater than that of other algorithms. The reason is that the LDPart algorithm perturbs every bit of the grid encoding results where the user is located, resulting in a wide range of differences between the perturbed location and the actual location. The GT-R algorithm randomly selects a layer of nodes in the quadtree index structure to carry out the random response perturbation. When the selected layer is close to the root node, the perturbation distance is far from the real location. The proposed LDPORR algorithm has a smaller average perturbation distance than the DPL-Hc algorithm and the LDPHE algorithm in most cases. However, when the privacy budget is very small, the Laplace noise introduced by the DPL-Hc algorithm is smaller than the perturbation generated by the random response mechanism. When the introduced perturbation is significantly large, the random response implemented on only one bit generates less error compared with the random response that happened on all the bits. That's why the LDPHE algorithm performs better than the proposed LDPORR algorithm when the privacy budget is very small.

4.5.4 Efficiency and Overhead

To evaluate the efficiency and overhead of the proposed LDPORR algorithm, we compare the execution time of the perturbation process of a single user and the volume of uploaded data (the amount of data submitted from the user side to the server side). For the sake of fairness, all the perturbation algorithms use the same spatial decomposition granularity, and each of the algorithms is executed 500 times to determine the average value of execution time. Experimental results are depicted in Figure 4.12 and Table 4.3.

It can be observed from Figure 4.12 that all the algorithms can finish the location privacy protection process for mobile users within a relatively short period. Among them, the GT-R algorithm has the longest execution time, the LDPart algorithm takes second place, and the execution time of other algorithms are similar. Combined with the uploaded data volume portrayed in Table 4.3, the primary reason is that

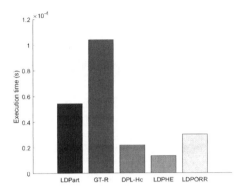

Figure 4.12 Comparison of execution time.

TABLE 4.3 Comparison of upload overhead.

Algorithm	Data volume (bit)
LDPart	N^2
GT-R	N^2
DPL-Hc	$2\lceil\log_2 N\rceil$
LDPHE	$2\lceil\log_2 N\rceil$
LDPORR	$2\lceil\log_2 N\rceil$

the GT-R algorithm and the LDPart algorithm have more data to upload after spacial decomposition and encoding. The GT-R algorithm needs to construct a quadtree index structure based on the grid partitioning granularity N. In the worst-case scenario, the GT-R algorithm may choose the leaf node layer and carry out the random response on N^2 bits of encodings. While the LDPart algorithm directly generates N^2 bits of encoding vectors according to the same grid partitioning granularity N. Therefore, the LDPart algorithm saves more time than the GT-R algorithm. The DPL-Hc, LDPHE, and LDPORR algorithms use the same Hilbert curve partitioning structure and receive the encoding vector of $2\lceil\log_2 N\rceil$ bits. The DPL-Hc algorithm incorporates Laplace noise into the encoding result, which is faster than the speed of random response of the proposed LDPORR algorithm. The LDPHE algorithm only selects one bit to carry out the random response perturbation, therefore, its operational efficiency is superior to other algorithms.

4.6 CONCLUSION

Location information is continuously collected and used in various popular application fields of big data, such as the Internet of Things, intelligent transportation, location-based services, mobile crowd-sensing, etc. It not only brings unprecedented convenience to our lives but also becomes a natural interface between individuals and the Internet. However, with the increased awareness of personal privacy and security among the public, the issue of location privacy protection has also attracted widespread attention. Local differential privacy location protection methods enable mobile users to independently process and protect their locations without reliance on third-party servers, which can provide more flexible and personalized location privacy protection effects. To solve the problems of complex encoding mechanisms, high communication costs, and low availability of current local differential privacy location protection methods, this chapter proposes a new solution based on the optimized random response. Dimension reduction and location encoding have been implemented using spatial decomposition and the Hilbert curve. An optimized random response mechanism is designed to improve the availability of perturbation results and the accuracy of data aggregation. It has been demonstrated that the proposed local differential privacy location protection method satisfies the definition of ε-LDP, and the excellence of the method in terms of location data availability and accuracy of data aggregation has been verified through experiments.

However, the study still has some limitations. Firstly, the spatial partition granularity is determined by the server side, which will increase the computation and communication costs for both the server and the user side if the partition granularity is too large, or result in excessive perturbation distance if the partition granularity is too small. Therefore, finding a way to balance computation and communication costs with the loss of service quality is one of our future objectives. Secondly, the proposed location perturbation algorithm on the user side implements the optimized random response on each bit of the Hilbert encoding. In some application circumstances, it is unable to satisfy the demands of various users for different levels of location privacy protection. Therefore, combining the personalized local differential privacy model to disturb different regions of Hilbert encoding is also a direction that can be further studied.

CHAPTER 5

Achieving Location Privacy Protection via Geo-Indistinguishability and Location Semantics

THE areas where humans work and live have different location semantics and sensitivities according to their different social functions. Although the privacy protection of users' real locations can be achieved by some perturbation algorithm, the attackers may employ the semantic information of the perturbed locations to infer users' real location semantic in an attempt to spy on users' privacy to certain extent. In order to mitigate the above semantic inference attack and further improve the quality of location-based services, this chapter hereby proposes a user-side location perturbation and optimization algorithm based on geo-indistinguishability and semantic. The perturbation area satisfying geo-indistinguishability is thus generated according to the planar Laplace mechanism and optimized by combining the semantic information and time characteristics of the location. The optimum perturbed location that is able to satisfy the minimum loss of location-based service quality is selected via a linear pro gramming method, and can be employed to replace the real location of the user so as to prevent the leakage of the privacy. Experimental comparison of the actual road network and semantic location dataset manifests that the local perturbed location generation and optimization algorithm envisaged in this chapter is superior to the other state-of-the-art location perturbation algorithms in terms of the loss of location-based service quality, availability of generated location, and privacy protection intensity.

5.1 INTRODUCTION

As a formal notion of privacy for location-based systems, the geo-indistinguishability model proposed by Andres *et al.* [162] protects the user's exact location while allowing approximate information to be released for obtaining certain desired services. In prac-

DOI: 10.1201/9781003546344-5

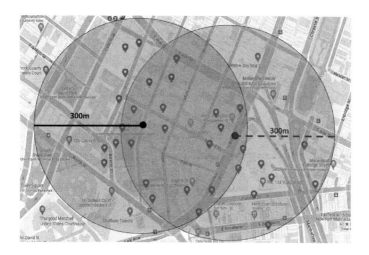

Figure 5.1 Location perturbation will lose LBS services outside the intersection area. (Geo-information obtained via Google Maps (https://www.google.com/maps/@40.7065085,-74.0114109,17.5z?entry=ttu), and the user's querying range and POI have been marked manually)

tical applications, location perturbation mechanism based on geo-indistinguishability needs to face the challenges from the following aspects. First of all, the perturbation mechanism needs to balance the quality loss of location-based services and location privacy leakage. If the distance between the perturbed location and the real location is too large, the quality of location-based services will be severely compromised. As depicted in Figure 5.1, the user wants to retrieve the points of interest within 300 meters of his or her real location. If the perturbed location submitted by the user is far away from the real one, the results returned by the LBS server may only contains a small part of the real points of interest (POI), which will greatly reduce users' experience of the LBS. On the contrary, if the distance between the perturbed location and the real location is too small, it may not able to prevent the leakage of location privacy and other related privacy.

Secondly, most of the existing perturbation mechanisms based on geo-indistinguishability are designed for location information in free space and do not consider the spatio-temporal rationality of the perturbed locations [163]. Perturbed locations that appear at unreasonable times and locations not only fail to protect location privacy, but may also attract the attention of attackers. For example, a user is on the coastal road to the airport, but the perturbation mechanism of free space generates a perturbation location in the sea, which is obviously unreasonable. Another example is that a user leaves the hospital where he/she works at 00:30 and is planning to take a taxi to go home. However, the semantic information of the perturbed location submitted to the LBS system is a nearby primary school. According to common sense in life, it is unlikely that there will be people in primary school at such a time. Therefore, the attacker can naturally rule out this fake location.

Besides, users are active in the real road network environment. The location areas with different social functions have different semantic information and sensitivity.

Usually, location semantics can be classified into different categories such as medical care, education, catering, entertainment, finance, transportation, etc. If the attacker has the background knowledge of the urban road network and related location semantic information, he can implement the semantic inference attack accordingly. For example, the user is reluctant to disclose his trip to the dental clinic, but his destination after perturbation shows that he is in the inpatient department of the hospital. Although the precise location information of the user is not exposed, the same semantic information still cannot prevent an attacker from inferring that the user has a health problem.

In order to solve the above problems, this chapter proposes a localized location perturbation and optimization algorithm based on geo-indistinguishability and semantics. The main contributions are as follows:

- A location perturbation generation algorithm is proposed based on geo-indistinguishability and location semantic which generates the optional regions for perturbed locations based on the planar Laplacian mechanism, and further optimizes the optional regions in accordance with the similarity and temporal correlation of location semantics.

- An optimal selection algorithm for the perturbed location is designed with the objective function to minimize the quality loss of the location-based service. The optimal perturbed location is selected from the optional regions by linear programming.

- Extensive experiments on real location datasets suggest that the location perturbation generation and optimization algorithm proposed in this chapter is superior in contrast to the other existing location perturbation mechanisms in terms of privacy protection strength and data availability.

5.2 STATE OF THE ART

To overcame the degradation of LBS service quality caused by the location K-anonymity model, Andres *et al.* proposed the concept of geo-indistinguishability [162]. This mechanism introduced controlled noise to the user's real location to obtain an approximate location and then sent it to the server to obtain the desired service. Within a circular region of radius r, the attacker can barely tell the difference between the approximate location and the real location. Takagi *et al.* [163] proposed the geo-graph-indistinguishability privacy protection mechanism based on the road network environment, which takes the road intersection as the perturbed location of user and improves the shortcomings of the geo-indistinguishability mechanism in the privacy and utility of the actual road network. Chatzikokolakis *et al.* [164] proposed two approaches to achieve geo-indistinguishability for generic locations and custom locations respectively, and extended the proposed mechanism to the case of location tracking. Yu *et al.* [165] demonstrated that geo-indistinguishability is ineffective against the optimal inference attacks and thus proposed a framework to adapt geo-indistinguishability to expected inference errors. Al-Dhubhani *et al.* [166] investigated the potential correlations between obfuscated locations generated according to geo-indistinguishability in continuous query services. Hua *et al.* [167] partitioned the planar location area into several hexagons and combined the geo-indistinguishability to reduce the loss of privacy parameters by publishing the location of the centroid of each hexagon. Qiu *et al.* [168] applied geo-indistinguishability to solve the problem of vehicle-based spatial crowdsourcing location privacy protection on road networks, and designed a location obfuscation strategy to reduce the quality loss caused by obfuscation. Arain *et al.* [169] propose an algorithm to protect the information of mobile vehicle's users and use geo-indistinguishability to obtain a set of POIs near the source location and destination location. Luo *et al.* [170] first classified the location set through a density-based clustering algorithm and then perturbed the real locations according to geo-indistinguishability so as to solve the problem of privacy leakage caused by frequent check-in. Xiong *et al.* [171] applied geo-indistinguishability to spatial crowdsourcing and combined location obfuscation and path optimization to provided strong privacy protection with minimal cost.

If attackers have obtained the background knowledge related to the anonymous space or perturbed location, especially the semantic information related to the location, the effect of anonymity and location perturbation will be seriously reduced. Therefore, many location privacy protection methods incorporate location semantics to enhance their protection effect. Xiao *et al.* [172] analyzed the problem that location K-anonymity suffers from query homogeneity attacks due to the lack of semantic diversity. They proposed a p-sensitive privacy-preserving model to realize location anonymity while considering query diversity and semantics. Lee *et al.* [173] suggested to learn semantic information from location data and let trusted anonymity servers perform location anonymization by hiding semantically heterogeneous locations. Agir *et al.* [174] introduced an inference model considering location semantics and semantic privacy-preserving mechanisms, and conducted a formal analysis of the bidirectional problem between semantic level and location inference. The PrivSem privacy protection framework proposed by Li *et al.* [175] integrates location K-anonymity, segmental-semantic diversity, and differential privacy to protect user's location privacy from infringing. Wang *et al.* [176] suggested to calculate the semantic distance and query probability between fake locations and build a location semantic tree to satisfy the semantic diversity. Kuang *et al.* [177] suggested to generate the sensitive weight document automatically according to the user's sensitivity to the semantics of different locations. Then, the K-anonymous optimal cooperative segment of the user's location is obtained through the reinforcement learning algorithm. Finally, user's location and query location have been perturbed based on the location semantics of the real road network environment. Bostanipour *et al.* [178] proposed a joint obfuscation algorithm based on mixing semantic label to solve the problem of privacy leakage that may occur in anonymous regions. Min *et al.* [179] designed a location perturbation strategy based on reinforcement learning, which adaptively selects perturbation strategy according to the sensitivity of semantic location. Xiao *et al.* [180] use differential privacy to protect a user data and use deep reinforcement learning to select a privacy parameter to achieve a balance between recommended service quality and privacy protection intensity.

5.3 PRIOR KNOWLEDGE

To achieve user-side location privacy protection, most approaches either generalize a user's exact location to a location region that includes other users in the vicinity, or randomly perturb the original location or its encoding to generate a fake location that can replace the original one. The above solutions not only increase the communication and data transmission overheads, but also severely degrade the quality of location-based services. Geo-indistinguishability is a formal notion of privacy for location-based systems, which formalizes the intuitive notion of protecting the user's location within a radius r with a level of privacy that depends on r, and corresponds to a generalized version of the well-known concept of differential privacy.

In order to facilitate the understanding of subsequent definitions and descriptions, we provide a unified explanation of the mathematical notations defined and employed in this chapter (as depicted in Table 5.1).

TABLE 5.1   Mathematical notations.

Symbol	Description
ε	Privacy budget
$d(x_1, x_2)$	Euclidean distance between any two locations x_1 and x_2
x_0	User's real location
x^*	The perturbed location
r	Distance between user's real location and perturbed location
θ	Polar angle
$f_\varepsilon(r, \theta)$	The probability density function in polar coordinates
D_i	Statistical vector of the ith location semantics
LS_{matrix}	Location semantic matrix
$CoS(D_a, D_b)$	The cosine similarity between two semantic location D_a and D_b
$\overline{CoS}$	Average semantic similarity
ρ	The lower limitation of the number of users
π_x	The prior probability of location x
$QL(P, \pi, d)$	Quality loss of LBS services (with perturbation matrix P, prior probability π, and distance d between the real and the perturbed locations
$p_{x_i x_j}$	Probability of perturbation from location x_i to location x_j
M_{dis}	The mean value of the distance between the real location and the perturbed location
V_{dis}	The variance of the distance between the real location and the perturbed location
RE	The relative error of range counting query

5.3.1 Geo-Indistinguishability

Definition 5.1 *Geo-indistinguishability [162]: For a finite set of possible locations $\mathcal{X}$ and a finite set of possible reported locations $\mathcal{Z}$, a perturbation mechanism K satisfies ε-geo-indistinguishability if for any two locations $x_1, x_2 \in \mathcal{X}$, $z \in \mathcal{Z}$, there is:*

$$K(x_1)(z) \le e^{\varepsilon d(x_1, x_2)} \cdot K(x_2)(z) \tag{5.1}$$

wherein, ε is the privacy budget, $d(x_1, x_2)$ represents the Euclidean distance between x_1 and x_2.

According to Definition 5.1, whenever the actual location of user $x_1 \in \mathcal{X}$, a perturbation mechanism K that satisfies ε-geo-indistinguishability will randomly generate and report a location $x_2 \in \mathcal{X}$, differs at most by a multiplicative factor $e^{\varepsilon d(x_1, x_2)}$. Therefore, it is impossible for potential attackers to determine the user's real location by observing the reported location set $\mathcal{Z}$ by the user. Location privacy has been protected on the user-side.

For a 2D planar location (with longitude and latitude coordinates), the geo-indistinguishability model generates a perturbed location in a probabilistic manner to replace the user's real location. Specifically, in a circular area centered on the user's real location, a perturbed location closer to the real one will be generated with a higher probability, while a perturbed location further away from the real one will be obtained with a lower probability (as depicted in Figure 5.2). Geo-indistinguishability can be seen as the generalized local differential privacy, which is an extension of the differential privacy model in two-dimensional space. For two different location points in the free space, there is a certain probability to perturb them onto a same point.

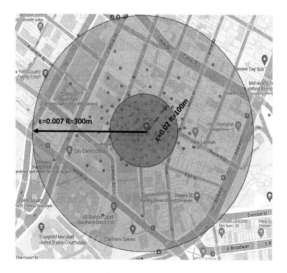

Figure 5.2 Distribution of perturbed locations generated according to geo-indistinguishability. (Geo-information obtained via Google Maps (https://www.google.com/maps/@40.7065085,-74.0114109,17.5z?entry=ttu), and the cover range of perturbed locations has been marked manually)

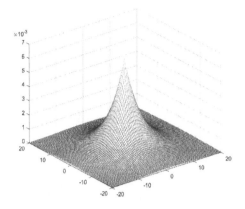

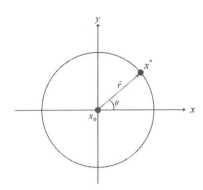

Figure 5.3 The probability density function of planar Laplace mechanism.

Figure 5.4 Planar Laplace mechanism in polar coordinates.

Considering that there is a certain distance between the two location points, a distance metric is introduced to the probability of perturbation to the same location point. Geo-indistinguishability can be seen as an enhanced version of local differential privacy with a distance metric. When $d(x_1, x_2) = 1$, geo-indistinguishability is equal to local differential privacy.

5.3.2 Plane Laplace Mechanism

The plane Laplace mechanism provides a method to generate noise so to satisfy geo-indistinguishability, which models the location domain as a discrete Cartesian plane with the standard notion of Euclidean distance. This model can be considered a good approximation of the Earth surface when the area of interest is not too large.

Definition 5.2 *Plane Laplace mechanism [162]: Let x_0 be the real location and x^* be the perturbed location, the probability density function of the planar Laplace mechanism can be expressed as:*

$$Lap^2 = \frac{\varepsilon^2}{2\pi}e^{-\varepsilon d(x_0, x^*)} \tag{5.2}$$

wherein $\frac{\varepsilon^2}{2\pi}$ is a normalization factor and ε is the privacy budget.

In order to facilitate the use of the plane Laplace mechanism to achieve geo-indistinguishability, the probability density function of the plane Laplace mechanism (portrayed in Figure 5.3) is converted into the probability density function in polar coordinates (depicted in Figure 5.4):

$$f_\varepsilon(r, \theta) = \frac{\varepsilon^2}{2\pi}re^{-\varepsilon r} \tag{5.3}$$

wherein r represents the distance between the real location x_0 and the perturbed location x^*, θ is the polar angle formed by the line x_0x^* with the horizontal axis of the polar coordinates.

The two random variables r and θ, representing radius and angle, are independent. Therefore, the probability density function of the planar Laplace mechanism [162] can be expressed as:

$$f_\varepsilon(r, \theta) = f_{\varepsilon,R}(r) f_{\varepsilon,\Theta}(\theta) \tag{5.4}$$

$$f_{\varepsilon,R}(r) = \int_0^{2\pi} f_\varepsilon(r, \theta) d\theta = \varepsilon^2 r e^{-\varepsilon r} \tag{5.5}$$

$$f_{\varepsilon,\Theta}(\theta) = \int_0^{\infty} f_\varepsilon(r, \theta) dr = \frac{1}{2\pi} \tag{5.6}$$

5.3.3 Location Semantics

Different geographic areas in a city provide different services and play different social roles for users, which is called the semantic information of location. Figure 5.5 portrays a simplified road network structure and its location semantics, wherein, H for hospital, S for school, and M for mall. Considering the different probability that each type of semantic may be visited, Damiani *et al.* [181] put forward the concept of popularity according to the different probabilities of accessing the location with different semantic type and uses it for the location semantic modeling.

We believe that users' frequency of appearance and duration of stay in different geographical areas portray the degree of the user's association with the semantic of the location, which in turn reflects users' habits and behavioural patterns. The attacker can infer the user's private information based on the semantic information of the user's location, which is called semantic inference attack. For different users, the semantic sensitivity of different locations is different, so the impact of privacy leakage caused by semantic inference attacks is also different. For example, for doctors and nurses working in hospitals, the leakage of location information of their workplace will not affect them much. They may be more concerned about the privacy of their home address. For ordinary users, on the other hand, they may be more concerned about the leakage of their location information when they are in the hospital, which can lead to semantic inference attacks on the privacy of their health status. In addition, the statistical properties of location semantics are closely related to time. The

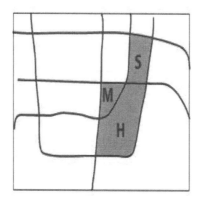

Figure 5.5 A simplified road network structure and its location semantics.

distributional characteristics of different location semantics are different at the same time. The statistical characteristics of the same location semantics also vary significantly in different time periods. For example, pubs, which are the main entertainment venues at night, always have more customers at night and fewer customers during daytime working hours. On the contrary, semantic locations such as banks, transport hubs, schools, etc. are always more crowded during working hours than during leisure time. We combine statistical features of location semantics with temporal relations to build a time-series representation of location semantics.

Definition 5.3 *Location semantic matrix: Let vector $D_i = [N_{i1}, \ldots, N_{ij}, \ldots, N_{it}]'$ be the statistical information of the ith location semantics at different time parameters, where N_{ij} is the number of people who appeared in the ith location semantic region during the jth time period. Therefore, the location semantic matrix of a city can be expressed as:*

$$LS_{matrix} = [D_1, D_2, \ldots, D_m] = \begin{bmatrix} N_{11} & N_{21} & \cdots & N_{m1} \\ N_{12} & N_{22} & \cdots & N_{m2} \\ \vdots & \vdots & \ddots & \vdots \\ N_{1t} & N_{2t} & \cdots & N_{mt} \end{bmatrix} \quad (5.7)$$

wherein, m represents the number of location semantic types in the city.

5.4 LOCATION PERTURBATION BASED ON GEO-INDISTINGUISHABILITY AND LOCATION SEMANTICS

Traditional localized differential privacy model (LDP) realizes the privacy protection of a user's data through random response mechanism. When a user's data consists of multiple parameters, the random response mechanism can be applied on each kind of parameter. However, this approach ignores the association between the parameters. Especially, the location information, the longitude information, or the latitude information cannot be analyzed in isolation as this would seriously damage the usability of the original location information.

Geo-indistinguishability can be seen as a generalized form of LDP, which is an extension of the differential privacy model in the 2D space. The definition of geo-indistinguishability (i.e., Definition 5.1) introduces a distance metric to the concept of local differential privacy. Algorithm satisfying geo-indistinguishability can return a perturbed location closer to the real location with a larger probability and a perturbed location farther from the real location with a smaller probability. Therefore, it is particularly suitable for localized differential privacy protection of location information. According to Eq. (5.1), the attacker can hardly tell the difference between the perturbed and the real locations within a circular area (which is controlled by the privacy parameter ε).

According to the plane Laplace mechanism in the polar coordinates, the user's real location x_0 can be perturbed into a fake one x' that satisfies geo-indistinguishability. In order to reduce the influence of the selection of the two random variables of radius and angle on the perturbed location, the average distance can be calculated by multiple iterations and used to represent the distance $d(x_0, x')$ between the perturbed location and the real location. Let the user's real location x_0 be the center of the circle, and the average distance generated by the plane Laplace mechanism be the radius, all the geo-indistinguished locations that satisfy user's privacy requirement ε constitute a perturbation area:

$$P_{area} = \{center = x_0, radius = \frac{1}{N} \times \sum_{i=1}^{N} r_i\} \qquad (5.8)$$

wherein N is the number of geo-indistinguished locations in the perturbation area.

Algorithm 5.1 depicts the pseudo-code of the perturbation area generation algorithm. Figure 5.6 portrays the perturbation areas corresponding to different privacy parameters ε. As the privacy parameter ε decreases, the perturbations introduced by the planar Laplace mechanism become larger and the coverage of the generated perturbed area becomes larger.

Considering that the location of the user when submitting the LBS service request has semantic information, if a perturbed location that satisfies geo-indistinguishability is randomly selected within the perturbed area generated by Algorithm 1, it is likely to appear that the perturbed location and the real location belong to the same location semantic type or location semantic types with high similarity. In order to prevent attackers from inferring users' location privacy based on the semantic information in the road network and the prior knowledge of users' distribution, this section proposes a perturbation area optimization algorithm based on location semantics. The location privacy perturbation area generated by Algorithm 1 will be filtered by removing perturbed locations that have too much semantic similarity to the real location and where the number of users at the current time is less than the threshold.

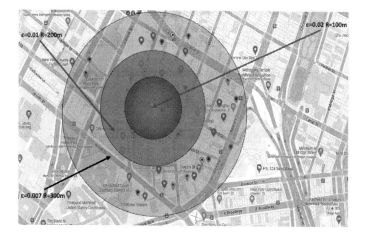

Figure 5.6 Variations of perturbation area with privacy parameter ε. (Geo-information obtained via Google Maps (https://www. google.com/maps/@40.7065085,-74.0114109,17.5z?entry=ttu), and corresponding perturbation areas have been marked manually)

Algorithm 5.1 Perturbation area generation algorithm

Input: User's real location x_0, privacy budget ε, parameter N

Output: Perturbation area P_{area}

1: $total\_dis = 0$

2: **for** i from 1 to N **do**

3:    $\theta \longleftarrow$ uniformly select in $[0, 2\pi)$

4:    $p \longleftarrow$ uniformly select in $[0, 1)$

5:    $r = C_\varepsilon^{-1}(p) = -\frac{1}{\varepsilon}(W_{-1}(\frac{p-1}{e}) + 1)$

6:    $x = x_0 + (r \cdot cos(\theta), r \cdot sin(\theta))$

7:    $total\_dis = total\_dis + d(x_0, x)$

8: **end for**

9: $R = \frac{total\_dis}{N}$

10: $P_{area} = \{center = x_0, radius = R\}$

Definition 5.4 *Location semantic similarity: Let D_a and D_b be the vectors of location semantics for locations a and b, the cosine similarity can be used to measure the similarity of these two location semantics.*

$$CoS(D_a, D_b) = \frac{\vec{D_a} \cdot \vec{D_b}}{\left|\vec{D_a}\right| \cdot \left|\vec{D_b}\right|} \tag{5.9}$$

If the cosine similarity value between two location semantics is closer to 1, it means that the similarity between the two location semantics is higher. Let N be the number of locations within the perturbation area, the average semantic similarity can be expressed as Eq. (5.10):

$$\overline{CoS} = \frac{1}{N} \times \sum_{i=1}^{N} CoS(D_{x_0}, D_{x_i}) \qquad x_0, x_i \in P_{area} \tag{5.10}$$

Let $N_t(x)$ be the number of people at location x on time t, and the lower limitation of the number of users be ρ. The proposed perturbation area optimization algorithm consists of two main phases: Firstly, the perturbed locations where the number of users is less than the lower limitation ρ will be removed. Because the perturbed locations with fewer users than the lower bound lack group masking effects and tend to reveal the presence of users. Secondly, the perturbed locations with higher semantic similarity than the average similarity will also be removed. Since these locations are semantically highly similar to the user's real location, it is easy for an attacker to infer the rest of the user's privacy using the location semantic features.

Algorithm 5.2 portrays the pseudocode of the perturbation area optimization algorithm based on location semantics. Figure 5.7 is the optimization result of the perturbed area obtained from Figure 5.6, in which different colors are used to represent interest points with different semantic information. According to the proposed definition of location semantic matrix, Algorithm 5.2 further eliminates the disturbed locations that have over threshold value of semantic similarity with the user's real location and do not meet the lower limitation of the number of users on the basis of Algorithm 5.1.

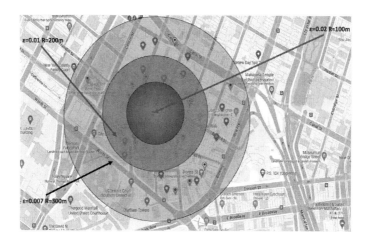

Figure 5.7 The optimized effect of perturbation area on the basis of Figure 5.6. (Geo-information obtained via Google Maps (https://www.google.com/maps/@40.7065085,-74.0114109,17.5z?entry=ttu), and corresponding perturbation areas have been marked manually)

5.5 OPTIMAL SELECTION ALGORITHM BASED ON LINEAR PROGRAMMING

In practical applications, attackers may collect and obtain the semantic information of the road network and the prior knowledge of users' distribution by different ways. These background knowledge may help them to infer users' location privacy. Let's consider the following scenario: there are 4 locations A, B, C, and D, and the attackers know that the number of people in A, B, C, and D is 10, 20, 30, and 40 respectively based on prior knowledge. Therefore, it can be considered that the prior probabilities of the users' real location in the above four locations are $\pi_A = 0.1$, $\pi_B = 0.2$, $\pi_C = 0.3$, and $\pi_D = 0.4$. So the attackers may infer that the user is in location D at the current time with a probability of 40%. Combining this phenomenon, it is easy to obvious that although Algorithm 5.2 has optimized the perturbed area with location semantics and has reduced the leakage of location semantic information, the problem of prior probability inference is still exists. Therefore, this section proposes an optimal selection algorithm for the perturbed locations based on Algorithm 5.2.

Definition 5.5 *Prior probability: The prior probability of location x within area $\mathcal{X}$ on time t can be expressed by the ratio of the number of people at a location x to the total number of people at all locations in $\mathcal{X}$.*

$$\pi_x = \frac{N_t(x)}{|\mathcal{X}|_t} \tag{5.11}$$

wherein $N_t(x)$ is the number of people at location x on time t and $\mathcal{X}_t$ manifests the total number of people at all locations in $\mathcal{X}$ at the same time.

Algorithm 5.2 Perturbation area optimization algorithm

Input: The user's real location x_0, perturbation area P_{area}, the lower limit of the number of users ρ, current time t

Output: Optimized area O_{area}

1: $O_{area} = P_{area}$
2: **for** each location x in O_{area} **do**
3:      **if** $N_t(x) < \rho$ **then**
4:          delete x from O_{area}
5:      **end if**
6: **end for**
7: Calculate $\overline{COS}$ for O_{area} according to Eq.(5.10)
8: **for** each location x in O_{area} **do**
9:      **if** $Cos(D_{x_0}, D_x) > \overline{COS}$ **then**
10:         delete x from O_{arca}
11:      **end if**
12: **end for**
13: **return** O_{area}

Definition 5.6 *Loss of QoS: Let π_x be the prior probability that the user is at location x, P is the perturbation matrix, $p_{x_0 x^*}$ stands for the probability of perturbation from original location x_0 to the perturbed location x^*, and $d(x_0, x^*)$ represents the Euclidean distance between x_0 and x^*. The service quality loss can be measured by:*

$$QL(P, \pi, d) = \sum\nolimits_{x_0, x^*} \pi_x \cdot p_{x_0 x^*} \cdot d(x_0, x^*) \tag{5.12}$$

In order to improve the LBS service quality obtained based on the perturbed location, the optimal selection algorithm proposed in this section constructs a linear programming function with the objective of minimizing the loss of service quality:

$$Minimize : QL(P, \pi, d) \tag{5.13}$$

$$Subject\ to \begin{cases} p_{x_0 z} \le e^{\varepsilon d(x_0, x^*)} \cdot p_{x^* z}, & \forall x_0, x^*, z \in \mathcal{X} \\ p_{x_0 z} \ge 0, & \forall x_0, z \in \mathcal{X} \\ \sum_{z \in \mathcal{X}} p_{x_0 z} = 1, & \forall x_0 \in \mathcal{X} \end{cases} \tag{5.14}$$

The parameter $\mathcal{X}$ used in the constraint conditions represents the set of all the locations in the finite space. The constraint conditions contain three aspects: firstly, the perturbed locations must satisfy geo-indistinguishability; secondly, the perturbation probability must be larger than 0; finally, the sum of all the perturbed location probabilities with respect to the real location x_0 must be 1.

If the optimized area contains n candidates, the linear programming function in Eq. (5.14) will receive a perturbation matrix $P_{n \times n}$ as shown in Eq. (5.15). Each of the element $p_{x_i x_j}$ in the perturbation matrix stands for the probability of perturbation from location x_i to location x_j.

$$P_{n\times n} = \begin{bmatrix} p_{x_0 x_0} & p_{x_0 x_1} & \cdots & p_{x_0 x_{n-1}} \\ p_{x_1 x_0} & p_{x_1 x_1} & \cdots & p_{x_1 x_{n-1}} \\ \vdots & \vdots & \ddots & \vdots \\ p_{x_{n-1} x_0} & p_{x_{n-1} x_1} & \cdots & p_{x_{n-1} x_{n-1}} \end{bmatrix} \tag{5.15}$$

It should be noticed that there is a certain probability to return user's real location according to the perturbation matrix $P_{n\times n}$. To a certain extent, this is determined by the privacy parameter ε. When the value of the privacy parameter ε is large, the error introduced by the Laplace mechanism is small, and the perturbed location is likely to return the user's original true location. In order to prevent this from happening, the value corresponding to user's real location in the row vector can be removed, and an optimal perturbed location can be returned according to other remaining probability values.

Algorithm 5.3 The optimal selection algorithm

Input: Optimized area O_{area}, the prior probability π_x of location x, the privacy parameter ε

Output: Optimal perturbation location x^*

1: Perturbation matrix $P_{n\times n} = 0$
2: Add constraints:
3: **for** each row i in P **do**
4:    $\sum_{j=0}^{n-1} p_{ij} = 1$
5: **end for**
6: $\forall\, p_{x_i x_j} \geq 0$
7: **for** each x in O_{area} **do**
8:   **for** each x^* in O_{area} **do**
9:     **for** each z in O_{area} **do**
10:      $p_{xz} \leq e^{\varepsilon \cdot d(x,x^*)} \cdot p_{x^* z}$
11:     **end for**
12:   **end for**
13: **end for**
14: Add constraints end
15: $Minimize : \sum_{x,x^* \in O_{area}} \pi_x \cdot p_{xx^*} \cdot d(x, x^*)$
16: $x^* \leftarrow$ According to the perturbation probability of the first row of P
17: **return** x^*

Algorithm 5.3 portrays the pseudocode of the optimal selection algorithm. For the optimized area O_{area} with n candidate locations, Algorithm 5.3 is primarily carried out in two stages. The first stage is to incorporate some constraints (lines 2-14), i.e., according to our proposed method, there are three constraints. The first one (lines 3-5) requires that the sum of each row in perturbation matrix P must be 1, implying that the sum of the probabilities of perturbing the original location x_i to all of the other possible locations must be 1. It needs to calculate all the elements within the matrix P and thus the computational complexity for this part is $O(n^2)$. The second constraint (line 6) mandates that each of the element $p_{x_i x_j}$ within the perturbation matrix P must be greater than 0. The computational complexity of this part is about $O(n)$. The third constraint (lines 7-13) ensures that the perturbed locations meet the requirement of geo-indistinguishability (as defined in Eq.(5.2)). To achieve this particular goal, three nested loops are required, and hence, the computational complexity of this part is of the order of $O(n^3)$. The second stage of the proposed algorithm is to minimize the objective function (line 15). According to Eq.(5.13), the proposed algorithm needs to traverse P when constructing the objective function. Therefore, the computational complexity of the second stage is $O(n^2)$. To sum up, the computational complexity of the proposed algorithm should be $O(n^3)$.

5.6 PRIVACY ANALYSIS

The envisaged location perturbation and optimization algorithm based on geo-indistinguishability and semantic aims at scenarios of requesting LBS services on locations with semantic information in the road network, which is very consistent with the applications of location-based big data in our real life. Suppose an attacker has obtained the following background knowledge:

- The attacker has the road network information of the city including the distribution of various semantic locations;

- The attacker can obtain the number and distribution of users at any time and in area that he needs but cannot identify a specific user from it;

- The attacker may capture the location information submitted by a user to the LBS platform.

The following will prove that the proposed location perturbation and optimization algorithm can provide geo-indistinguished local differential privacy protection for a user's location and resist the semantic inference attack at the same time.

Proof: Our proposed solution consists of three algorithms. Firstly, the perturbation area will be generated by using Algorithm 5.1 according to a user's real location x_0 and privacy parameter ε. Then, the perturbation area will be optimized via Algorithm 5.2 based on the similarity and temporal correlation of location semantics. Finally, the optimal perturbed location will be selected via Algorithm 5.3 by using a linear programming function.

Let x_0 be the real location of a user, x^* indicates the perturbed location generated by the proposed perturbation and optimization algorithm K, and x_i represents any point within the perturbation area P_{area}. According to the definition of geo-indistinguishability depicted in Eq. (5.1), here is:

$$Pr[K(x_0) = x^*] \leq e^{\varepsilon \cdot d(x_0, x^*)} \cdot Pr[K(x^*) = x^*]$$
$$Pr[K(x_0) = x_i] \leq e^{\varepsilon \cdot d(x_0, x_i)} \cdot Pr[K(x_i) = x_i]$$

$$\frac{Pr[K(x_0) = x^*]}{Pr[K(x_0) = x_i]} \leq \frac{e^{\varepsilon \cdot d(x_0, x^*)} \cdot Pr[K(x^*) = x^*]}{e^{\varepsilon \cdot d(x_0, x_i)} \cdot Pr[K(x_i) = x_i]}$$

$$\leq \frac{e^{\varepsilon \cdot d(x_0, x^*)}}{e^{\varepsilon \cdot d(x_0, x_i)}}$$

$$= e^{\varepsilon \cdot (d(x_0, x^*) - d(x_0, x_i))}$$

$$\leq e^{\varepsilon \cdot d(x^*, x_i)}$$

$$\therefore Pr[K(x_0) = x^*] \leq e^{\varepsilon \cdot d(x^*, x_i)} \cdot Pr[K(x_0) = x_i]$$
$$\therefore Pr[K(x^*) = x_0] \leq e^{\varepsilon \cdot d(x^*, x_i)} \cdot Pr[K(x_i) = x_0]$$

Therefore, for any perturbed location within the perturbation area P_{area}, the proposed perturbation area generation algorithm (i.e., Algorithm 5.1) can provide geo-indistinguished local differential privacy protection for a user's location.

In Algorithm 5.2, the lower limit of the number of users ρ have been set up. During the optimization process, all of the perturbed locations having the same semantics as the real location and the ones having greater semantic similarity than the threshold are deleted. Meanwhile, the perturbed locations possessing the number of users less than ρ within the same time are also eliminated. This implies that the perturbed locations finally obtained by Algorithm 5.2 have less semantic similarities with their corresponding real locations and that the attacker cannot obtain the real semantics of the users' location, and it is impossible to further infer other privacy of the users according to their location semantics. Moreover, the setting of the lower limit of the number of users ρ ensures that the perturbed locations obtained by Algorithm 5.2 have the group masking effect so that the attacker cannot infer the real location of a user by means of the number and distribution of users at the corresponding moment.

In summary, the location perturbation and optimization algorithm proposed in this chapter can provide localized privacy protection for users' location and resist the semantic inference attack at the same time.

5.7 EXPERIMENTAL RESULTS AND PERFORMANCE ANALYSIS

In order to evaluate and analyze the location perturbation and optimization algorithm (marked as POLS) proposed in this chapter, we compare it with a number of classical perturbation mechanisms from the aspects of LBS service quality loss, privacy protection strength, and range counting query accuracy. The baseline methods include, but are not limited to, local differential privacy perturbation mechanism (marked as KRR) [183], geo-indistinguishability-based planar Laplace perturbation mechanism (marked as PL) [162], geometric perturbation mechanism (marked as GEOM) [184], and exponential perturbation mechanism (marked as EM) [185].

Use *Groubi* to perform the linear programming operations. The dataset used for the experiments includes 573,703 pieces of check-in information in Tokyo, Japan [182] from April 12, 2012 to February 16, 2013. Each piece of the check-in information contains GPS coordinates, timestamp, and the semantic information, which is used to study the spatiotemporal regularity of users' activities in LBSNs. We randomly select three sets of location points with scales of 50,000, 100,000, and 500,000 from the experimental dataset as the users' real locations. The distribution characteristics of the same location semantic at different times are significantly different. Therefore, we implement three groups of experiments at 03:00, 12:00, and 18:00 respectively. During the experiments, the lower limitation of the number of users is $\rho = 30$, and privacy parameter $\varepsilon \in \{0.004, 0.005, 0.007, 0.01, 0.02\}$.

5.7.1 Loss of QoS

In this section, the mean value and variance of the distance between the perturbed location and the real location are used to measure the loss of location-based service quality caused by different perturbation mechanisms. The definitions are depicted in the following Eq.(5.16) and Eq.(5.17).

$$M_{dis} = \frac{1}{N} \times \sum_{i=1}^{N} dis(x_i, x_i')$$
(5.16)

$$V_{dis} = \frac{1}{N} \times \sum_{i=1}^{N} (dis_i - M_{dis})^2$$
(5.17)

Figure 5.8 compares the mean distances of different perturbation mechanisms under various privacy parameters using the logarithmic coordinates. Figure 5.9 further compares the variance of the distance between the perturbed location and the real location, which can facilitate comparing the degree of variation in the perturbed distance produced by different perturbation mechanisms. Analyzing the above results we can observe that the mean value and variance of the distance between the perturbed location and the real location generated by the KRR algorithm are significantly higher than those of other algorithms and is hardly varies with the change of privacy parameters. The main reason is that the KRR algorithm has the same probability of all location points in the entire geospace being selected as the perturbed location when randomly responding to the user's real location based on the local

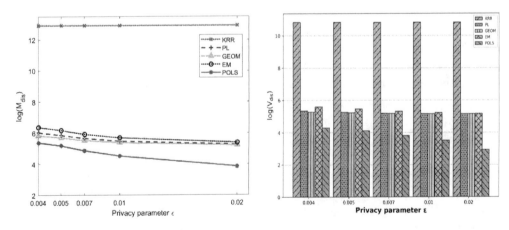

Figure 5.8 Comparison of M_{dis}.   Figure 5.9 Comparison of V_{dis}.

differential privacy model. The change of the privacy parameter ε will only affect the probability that the user's real location be selected to be the perturbed location, but will not make significant changes on the distance between the perturbed location and the real one. If the random response adopted by the KRR algorithm occurs on the higher bits of the latitude and longitude of users' location, the deviation of the disturbed location from the real location will be large, resulting in a surge of loss of quality for location-based services.

Combining the results in Figure 5.8 and Figure 5.9 we can observe that the mean value and the variance of the distance generated by PL, GEOM, and EM mechanism are relatively close, and they all gradually decrease with the increase of the privacy parameter ε. The reason is that the perturbation probability functions of the above three mechanisms are different, the same privacy parameter ε achieve different perturbation probabilities in the PL, GEOM, and EM algorithms and result in different perturbed distances. The same privacy parameter ε obtains more amount of perturbations while using the EM algorithm, therefore, the corresponding perturbed distance is farther and the mean value and the variance of the distance are larger than others.

The proposed POLS algorithm obtains the radius of the perturbed area corresponding to certain privacy parameter ε based on the geo-indistinguishability mechanism, and restricts all the possible perturbed locations within this area to limit the variation range of the mean value and variance of the perturbed distance. Therefore, the mean value and the variance of perturbed distance of the proposed POLS method are lower than other algorithms during various time periods, and the generated perturbed locations can provide better service quality for LBS system.

5.7.2 Privacy Protection Intensity

The attackers may intercept LBS requests submitted by users and infer additional privacy based on location information. The smaller the semantic correlation between the perturbed location generated by the local perturbation mechanism and the user's real location, the less likely the attackers can infer the users' privacy. Therefore, we use the cosine similarity between the perturbed location and the real location to evaluate the privacy protection intensity of different perturbation mechanisms. The calculation method of cosine similarity is defined in Eq.(5.9).

Figure 5.10 depicts the distribution ratio of the cosine similarity between the perturbed location and the real location generated by different perturbation mechanisms on the experimental dataset at 12:00 p.m. Since the setting of the privacy parameter has no effect on the distribution ratio of the cosine similarity, we only take $\varepsilon = 0.02$ as an example for analysis. Each of the ring in Figure 5.10 represents a perturbation mechanism and different colors stand for the distribution ratio of the cosine similarity between the perturbed location and the real location. It can be observed that in addition to the proposed POLS algorithm, the cosine similarity between the perturbed location and the real location generated by other algorithms is mainly distributed within the interval [0.8, 1]. As mentioned above, a higher cosine similarity means that the perturbed location has a higher semantic similarity with

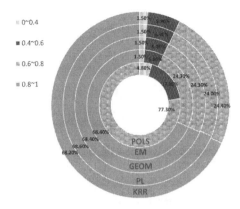

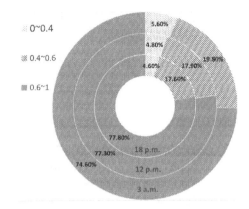

Figure 5.10 Distribution ratio of cosine similarity.

Figure 5.11 Cosine similarity of POLS algorithm.

the real location. Although the attackers may not directly obtain the users' precise location, they can analyze the users' behaviours, hobbies, habits, and many other privacy information according to the location semantics. On the contrary, the cosine similarity of the proposed POLS algorithm is mainly distributed within the interval [0.6, 0.8]. The proportion of the cosine similarity less than 0.6 reaches 22.7%, which is much higher than the level about 7% for other algorithms. The results proved that the perturbed location generated by the proposed POLS algorithm has lower semantic similarity with the real location, which facilitate to resist semantic inference attacks and provide users with better location privacy protection.

Figure 5.11 further compares the distribution ratio of the cosine similarity between the perturbed location and the real location generated by the proposed POLS algorithm in different time periods under the premise of the same privacy parameter ($\varepsilon = 0.02$). Although the number of users distributed on different semantic locations at different times is quite different, the proposed POLS algorithm can overcome the temporal difference of semantic location distribution and provide more consistent perturbation location generation effects in different time periods.

5.7.3 Availability of Perturbed Location

Location-based big data services collect and organize location information from various terminals and channels, and provide users with services such as inquiry of points of interest within a certain range, the number of other users, the number of available vehicles, traffic conditions, etc. In this section, the accuracy of the range counting query service is used to measure the availability of perturbed location data submitted by users. For a certain query range, the relative error (RE) between the real location dataset and the perturbed location dataset can be calculated according to the Eq. (3.18) in Chapter 3. The experiments randomly generated three different scales of location datasets within the area of city Tokyo at 12:00 p.m., when the users' activity patterns were the most abundant. The corresponding perturbed location datasets are obtained by performing different perturbation algorithms on the three original

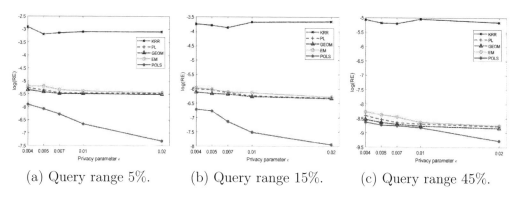

(a) Query range 5%. (b) Query range 15%. (c) Query range 45%.

Figure 5.12 Comparison of range counting query accuracy (dataset with 50,000 users).

location datasets mentioned above. Three sizes of spatial query ranges are set, which cover 5%, 15%, and 45% of the spatial area of the real location dataset respectively. Each of the query was randomly selected and executed for 10,000 times to determine the average relative error.

Figures 5.12-5.14 portray the relative error comparison results of various algorithms on different datasets in logarithmic scale. From the macro comparison of three location datasets of different sizes, the relative error of the range counting query gradually reduced with the increase of the number of users. The reason is that when the overall number of users is small, the distribution is relatively sparse and the change of users' location may lead to large deviations in the statistical results in a local area. As the overall number of users increases, the distribution density is also increases. The location change of some users takes them out of their original local area, while the location change of other users may bring them into this local area. Therefore, this kind of mutual cancellation reduces the bias of the range counting statistics. On the same location dataset, the relative error is also decreased as the query range increases from small area to large area. The main reason is that when the query range is small, some local users leave the current range after the location perturbation, resulting in a high relative error of the range counting query. With the increase of the query range,

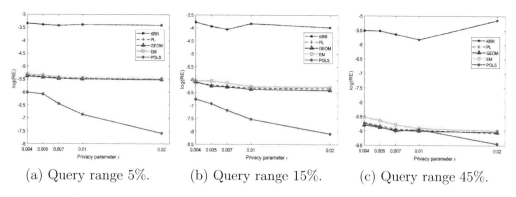

(a) Query range 5%. (b) Query range 15%. (c) Query range 45%.

Figure 5.13 Comparison of range counting query accuracy (dataset with 100,000 users).

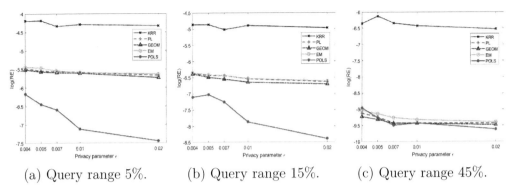

(a) Query range 5%.   (b) Query range 15%.   (c) Query range 45%.

Figure 5.14 Comparison of range counting query accuracy (dataset with 500,000 users).

the perturbation results of users' location may deviate from their original area, but it seldom exceed the query range, therefore, the relative error of the range counting query is also reduced.

When we compare the relative error of various location perturbation algorithms under the same dataset and query range, it can be observed that the relative error of the KRR algorithm does not change significantly with the change of the privacy parameters ε. Since the random response technology adopted by KRR algorithm is not directly related to the degree of location perturbation and the change of privacy parameter. The relative errors of the other algorithms gradually decrease with the increase of the privacy parameter ε. The reason is that the increase of the privacy parameter ε will reduce the incorporated perturbation value, so that the error between the published location and the real location also decreased. The proposed location perturbation and optimization algorithm aims at minimizing the quality loss of location-based services. The constructed service quality loss function comprehensively considers the distance between the perturbed location and the real location as well as the prior probability of users distribution. The above factors facilitate to constrain the users' perturbed location within a reasonable range. Therefore, the proposed location perturbation and optimization algorithm achieves better query accuracy than the other algorithms on datasets of various scales and with different privacy parameters. In the case of a small query range, the range counting query accuracy improvement of the proposed algorithm is more significant.

5.8 CONCLUSIONS

Aiming at the problem that adversary in a road network environment may infer users' location privacy based on the location semantics, this chapter proposes an end-user oriented location perturbation and optimisation method. The proposed method generates a perturbed location area conforming to geo-indistinguishability based on the planar Laplace mechanism, optimizes the perturbed location area using the average similarity of the location semantics, and selects the optimal perturbed location through a linear programming method. The proposed method not only achieves location privacy through geo-indistinguishability model but also protects location sensitivity through location semantics. Therefore, it can be extended and applied to trajectory privacy protection, avoiding semantic inference attacks by adversaries. Comparing with other location perturbation mechanisms, the proposed method has better performances in terms of quality loss of services, range query error, and privacy protection intensity.

CHAPTER 6

Conclusion

Location-based big data services enable consumers to form larger and closer links with the outside world. As networking, data, and intelligence become irreversible trends in digital society and business, personal data and privacy protection have become an ever-present issue throughout the life cycle of digital industry. Savage and rough industrial development not only harms people's enjoyment of the magnificent fruits of big data and information technology, but also stifles the long-term development of the digital industry. It has been demonstrated that in an era of more severe worldwide privacy protection rules, whomever can make excellent use of data and maximize its value while maintaining data security and personal privacy will be able to gain an advantage and stand out from the competitors.

6.1 SUMMARY OF THE CONTENTS

Taking location-based big data as a perspective, this book analyses the sources, characteristics and typical application areas of location big data. It provides an in-depth analysis of the privacy issues that may be raised by location big data and location-based services, as well as a review of the key existing approaches of location privacy protection and their performances. The results of the authors' and their team's work in the areas of privacy-preserving location information collection and statistical publishing and privacy protection of location big data are discussed at the technical level.

Specifically, the proposed differential privacy release method based on adaptive sampling and grid clustering adjustment is introduced to address the privacy leakage problem that may arise from the dynamic statistical publishing of location big data. The PID control strategy is combined with the data variation difference in the neighbouring release time to achieve the dynamic adjustment of the release time of location big data statistics. The temporal and spatial correlation of adjacent data snapshots is used to design the grid clustering and adjustment algorithm for location big data statistical release, which significantly improves the execution efficiency of the release algorithm. The differential privacy budget allocation strategy is improved to form a sliding window-based differential privacy statistical release algorithm, which achieves continuous statistical release and privacy protection and improves the accuracy of released data. Experiments and analysis demonstrate the advantages of the

DOI: 10.1201/9781003546344-6

proposed method in terms of the accuracy of adaptive sampling time, the availability of released data and the execution efficiency of the data release method.

In order to overcome the dependence of the centralized differential privacy model on third-party platforms and to further improve privacy protection during location big data collection, the proposed localized differential privacy location protection method based on optimized random response is presented. The designed spatial decomposition and encoding mechanism based on Hilbert curves can convert two-dimensional location data into one-dimensional Hilbert coding results. The proposed localized differential privacy location perturbation method based on optimized random response improves the accuracy of the perturbed locations after aggregation. Experiments on real location datasets demonstrate the advantages of the proposed method in terms of loss of location quality of service, availability of aggregated data, and efficiency of algorithm operation.

In order to prevent attackers from inferring users' real location semantics and further prying into users' privacy based on the semantic information of the perturbed location, the proposed localized location perturbation method that combines location semantics with geo-indistinguishability is introduced. The proposed method generates a perturbation region that satisfies geo-distinguishability based on the planar Laplace mechanism, and then optimizes the perturbation region based on the semantic information of users' real location and temporal features. Finally, the optimal perturbation location that can satisfy the minimum loss of the location-based quality of service can be filtered out by a linear programming method, which will be used as a substitute for the user's real location in order to prevent privacy leakage. Experimental comparisons of real road networks and semantic location datasets prove that the proposed method has certain advantages in terms of the loss of location-based quality of service, the availability of generated locations and the strength of privacy protection.

6.2 UNRESOLVED ISSUES AND CHALLENGES

To solve the problem of location privacy leakage in LBS, many novel countermeasures and solutions have been proposed by scholars at home and abroad. However, there are still some unresolved issues and research challenges that need to be further explored and discussed.

(1) Measurable problem with privacy-preserving mechanisms. There are different privacy metrics and methods available in LBS to evaluate the privacy-preserving performance of different location privacy-preserving mechanisms. Examples include K-anonymity, entropy, error-based estimators, ε-differential privacy, et al. However, the majority of them are customized to certain systems and attack models, making it difficult to use these metrics in a universal context. For the common user, over-specialized metrics lack the possibility line and flexibility for practical usage. As a result, identifying the appropriate and succinct privacy metrics to assess the efficacy of location privacy-preserving mechanisms is a major challenge.

(2) Problems caused by the great dimensionality and immediacy of location data. The great majority of current location privacy protection approaches only address

two-dimensional location data. However, as humans continue to explore places such as space and the ocean, large amounts of spatial and underwater location data have been acquired. Research into privacy protection for such high-dimensional geographical data has significant application value. Furthermore, LBS is a typical instant online application. The LBS server is regularly confronted with a high number of moving objects, ongoing service requests, and rapidly updated location information. How to create appropriate privacy protection solutions based on the high dimensionality and immediacy of location data? How to improve the performance and response speed of LBS processors so that consumers receive satisfactory online service results? All of these are worthwhile areas to pursue.

(3) The trade-off between privacy, service quality, and resource consumption. Privacy protection is predicated on the assumption that it incurs a cost, which can be measured in terms of data availability, network bandwidth, and effort by the user or the service provider. For example, data availability is a cost in location privacy protection approaches that rely on data distortion. The more accurate the data, the greater the availability, but the lower the privacy. Another example is the cost of redundant network traffic based on perturbed location or redundant query results after privacy protection. Therefore, how to balance the combined impact of LBS on privacy, service quality, and resource consumption remains an important open problem.

6.3 OUTLOOK FOR DEVELOPMENT TRENDS

In recent years, technologies such as quantum computing, artificial intelligence, blockchain, and edge computing have made great progress. The emergence of new computing architectures and intelligent algorithms has enabled the successful integration and deep mining of large volumes of locations, maps, and location-related data. We select privacy computing and blockchain as representatives of these technologies to analyze and anticipate the new advancements that these emerging technologies may bring to location-based big data, location-based services, as well as location privacy protection.

(1) Privacy Computing + Location Protection

Data, as a key production ingredient, has become a fundamental strategic resource and plays a pivotal role in the digital economy. The general process of AI empowering socioeconomic growth include analyzing, calculating, and training data in order to generate intelligent models and build intelligent systems capable of making intelligent and exact decisions. However, data processing involves the collection, storage, usage, processing, transfer, and distribution of data, which poses dangers and concerns in terms of data security and privacy leakage. On the one hand, the privacy leakage necessitates the support of data elements; on the other hand, data owners are hesitant to open up data sharing owing to personal privacy and other concerns, resulting in data silos. The efficient use of data and privacy protection has become a prominent contradiction.

Privacy-preserving computing is a critical theory and technology created to address this paradox and fulfill the objective of availability and invisibility of data

[38,186]. It is a set of technological systems that analyze and calculate data while protecting privacy in order to achieve data value mining and decision-making tasks. On the one hand, privacy-preserving computing can protect the privacy information contained in the data, while on the other hand, it can perform sufficient computation or processing of the data to form intelligent and precise decision-making and applications, breaking the data island, accelerating data circulation, and releasing the value of the data, which is the important goal and main content of privacy-preserving computing. This includes both homomorphic encryption [101,102] and zero-knowledge proof [187] based on cryptography, as well as differential privacy [82,83] and federated learning [188,189] that have been rapidly developed in recent years. The combination of the aforementioned methodologies with location privacy protection techniques can safeguard users' location privacy during location big data analysis and model training while allowing for data sharing and model improvement.

- *Decentralized data training and distributed model aggregation*: Federated learning allows data owners to keep their local data while numerous participants collaborate to train models without sharing data, exchanging training parameters only at intermediate stages. This new machine learning paradigm ensures that participants have control over the data while preventing direct leakage of user location information. Model parameters can be aggregated among the participants to achieve global update of the model.

- *Encrypted computing*: Using encrypted computing techniques such as homomorphic encryption or secure multi-party computing for location data processing and analysis ensures that location-based big data services have the desired effect without exposing users' real locations [190,191].

- *Differential privacy*: Differential privacy techniques enable data analysis while maintaining users' privacy. By adding noise or perturbation to the data, it can ensure that individual users' data is not identifiable, hence maintaining their location privacy.

(2) Blockchain + Location Privacy

Location privacy protection models for location-based services can be classified into two categories: centralized and distributed. The centralized location privacy protection model relies on the so-called trustworthy third-party (TTP). However, TTP may become a bottleneck of system performance and a target of network attacks, resulting in the direct leakage of a large amount of users' private information and irreversible losses if it is compromised. Furthermore, it is difficult to provide a completely trustworthy third-party server in practical applications, and many information security problems are triggered by third-party servers actively stealing and leaking users' important information. The distributed location privacy protection model can be implemented by individuals creating anonymous/obfuscated zones on their own or collectively. However, it does not account for users' self-interested and malicious behaviours in the actual world. For example, when collaborating to construct an anonymous zone, some people may reveal the real locations of others to malicious entities in order to reap further benefits. Users participating in the collaboration provide bogus locations to the requesting users, which may result in an anonymous zone that does not match the users' service quality and privacy protection requirements. When a malicious user pretends as an honest one and joins a collaboration group, the others are directly exposed to the risk of privacy leakage. Therefore, there is an urgent need for a technical means to regulate the actions of third-party servers and users in order to prevent privacy breaches while improving service quality.

As an emerging technology that changes traditional business structures and forms of social organization, blockchain has been employed in a variety of industries such as financial services, supply chain management, identity authentication, and data security. Many features of blockchain, such as decentralization, non-tampering, transparency, privacy protection, and programmability, coincide with the location privacy protection needs of LBS services [192,193].

- Blockchain is a distributed database in which data is kept on numerous nodes in a network and the nodes collaborate to preserve and verify the integrity of the data. This decentralized organizational structure can effectively fight against the failure, theft and intrusion of third-party servers in the centralized location privacy protection model.

- Blockchain ensures data security and integrity through the use of encryption technologies and consensus mechanisms. Once the data is recorded on the blockchain, it is almost impossible to tamper with or modify, which contributes to the integrity and reliability of location information and service data in the LBS system.

- The chained storage structure of blockchain assures information traceability, and it is utilized to preserve historical information regarding user and server interactions in LBS systems so that authorities have the ability to track and investigate malicious users.

- Blockchain can create a decentralized trust mechanism to promote cooperation and information sharing among users in LBS systems, reducing collaboration costs and user trust risks.

Bibliography

[1] Sagiroglu S, Sinanc D. Big data: A review. IEEE International conference on collaboration technologies and systems (CTS), 2013, 42-47.

[2] Chen M, Mao S, Liu Y. Big data: A survey. Mobile Networks and Applications, 2014, 19: 171-209.

[3] Chen C L P, Zhang C Y. Data-intensive applications, challenges, techniques and technologies: A survey on Big Data. Information sciences, 2014, 275: 314-347.

[4] Ge M, Bangui H, Buhnova B. Big data for internet of things: a survey. Future Generation Computer Systems, 2018, 87: 601-614.

[5] Oussous A, Benjelloun F Z, Lahcen A A, et al. Big Data technologies: A survey. Journal of King Saud University-Computer and Information Sciences, 2018, 30(4): 431-448.

[6] https://www.visualcapitalist.com/order-from-chaos-how-big-data-will-change-the-world/

[7] https://www.nature.com/news/2008/080903/pdf/455008a.pdf

[8] https://www.science.org/toc/science/331/6018

[9] Manyika J, Chui M, Brown B, et al. Big data: The next frontier for innovation, competition. Technical report, McKinsey Global Institute,, 2011.

[10] Kim G H, Trimi S, Chung J H. Big-data applications in the government sector. Communications of the ACM, 2014, 57(3): 78-85.

[11] Al Nuaimi E, Al Neyadi H, Mohamed N, et al. Applications of big data to smart cities. Journal of Internet Services and Applications, 2015, 6(1): 1-15.

[12] Vassakis K, Petrakis E, Kopanakis I. Big data analytics: Applications, prospects and challenges. Mobile big data: A roadmap from models to technologies, 2018, 3-20.

[13] Lee J G, Kang M. Geospatial big data: challenges and opportunities. Big Data Research, 2015, 2(2): 74-81.

[14] Deng X, Liu P, Liu X, et al. Geospatial big data: New paradigm of remote sensing applications. IEEE Journal of Selected Topics in Applied Earth Observations and Remote Sensing, 2019, 12(10): 3841-3851.

[15] Yin J, Dong J, Hamm N A S, et al. Integrating remote sensing and geospatial big data for urban land use mapping: A review. International Journal of Applied Earth Observation and Geoinformation, 2021, 103: 102514.

[16] Huang H, Yao X A, Krisp J M, et al. Analytics of location-based big data for smart cities: Opportunities, challenges, and future directions. Computers, Environment and Urban Systems, 2021, 90: 101712.

[17] https://www.chinairn.com/news/20231027/172954844.shtml

[18] https://airsage.com/

[19] Shi Q, Abdel-Aty M. Big data applications in real-time traffic operation and safety monitoring and improvement on urban expressways. Transportation Research Part C: Emerging Technologies, 2015, 58: 380-394.

[20] D'Alconzo A, Drago I, Morichetta A, et al. A survey on big data for network traffic monitoring and analysis. IEEE Transactions on Network and Service Management, 2019, 16(3): 800-813.

[21] Dwork C, Kenthapadi K, McSherry F, et al. Our data, ourselves: Privacy via distributed noise generation. Advances in Cryptology-EUROCRYPT 2006: 24th Annual International Conference on the Theory and Applications of Cryptographic Techniques, St. Petersburg, Russia, 2006, 486-503.

[22] Jain P, Gyanchandani M, Khare N. Big data privacy: a technological perspective and review. Journal of Big Data, 2016, 3: 1-25.

[23] Mehmood A, Natgunanathan I, et al. Protection of big data privacy. IEEE Access, 2016, 4: 1821-1834.

[24] Choi J P, Jeon D S, Kim B C. Privacy and personal data collection with information externalities. Journal of Public Economics, 2019, 173: 113-124.

[25] Ribeiro-Navarrete S, Saura J R, Palacios-Marques D. Towards a new era of mass data collection: Assessing pandemic surveillance technologies to preserve user privacy. Technological Forecasting and Social Change, 2021, 167: 120681.

[26] Narayanan A, Shmatikov V. Robust de-anonymization of large sparse datasets. IEEE Symposium on Security and Privacy, Oakland, CA, USA, 2008, 111-125.

[27] Tene O, Polonetsky J. Big data for all: Privacy and user control in the age of analytics. North Western Journal of Technology and Intellectual Property, 2012, 11: 239.

[28] Tucker C E. Social networks, personalized advertising, and privacy controls. Journal of Marketing Research, 2014, 51(5): 546-562.

[29] Srinivasan D. The antitrust case against Facebook: A monopolist's journey towards pervasive surveillance in spite of consumers' preference for privacy. Berkeley Bus. LJ, 2019, 16: 39.

[30] Schuitemaker R, Xu X. Product traceability in manufacturing: A technical review. Procedia CIRP, 2020, 93: 700-705.

[31] Warren S D, Brandeis L D. The Right to Privacy. Harvard Law Review, 1890.

[32] https://en.wikipedia.org/wiki/Privacy

[33] Westin A F. Privacy and freedom. Washington and Lee Law Review, 1968, 25(1): 166.

[34] Ku R S R. Cyberspace law: Cases and materials. Aspen Publishing, 2020.

[35] Intersoft Consulting. General data protection regulation. https://gdpr-info.eu/

[36] Zhu L, Liu Z J, Han S. Deep leakage from gradients. In: Advances in Neural Information Processing Systems. MIT Press, 2019. 14774-14784.

[37] Song C, Ristenpart T, Shmatikov V. Machine learning models that remember too much. In: Proc. of the 2017 ACM SIGSAC Conf. on Computer and Communications Security. ACM, 2017. 587-601.

[38] Lu R, Zhu H, Liu X, et al. Toward efficient and privacy-preserving computing in big data era. IEEE Network, 2014, 28(4): 46-50.

[39] Schiller J, Voisard A. Location-Based Services. Elsevier, 2004.

[40] Kupper A. Location-Based Services: Fundamentals and Operation. John Wiley & Sons, 2005.

[41] Schilit B N, Theimer M M. Disseminating active map information to mobile hosts. IEEE Network, 1994, 8(5): 22-32.

[42] Uphaus P O, Beringer B, Siemens K, et al. Location-based services–the market: success factors and emerging trends from an exploratory approach. Journal of Location Based Services, 2021, 15(1): 1-26.

[43] Sadoun B, Al-Bayari O. LBS and GIS technology combination and applications. IEEE/ACS International Conference on Computer Systems and Applications. IEEE, 2007: 578-583.

[44] Aloudat A, Michael K, Abbas R. Location-based services for emergency management: A multi-stakeholder perspective. International Conference on Mobile Business. IEEE, 2009: 143-148.

[45] Aloudat A, Michael K, Chen X, et al. Social acceptance of location-based mobile government services for emergency management. Telematics and informatics, 2014, 31(1): 153-171.

[46] Ragia L, Deriaz M. Location based services for traffic management. Advanced Systems Group (ASG), Geneva, 2006.

[47] Lee W H, Tseng S S, Shieh J L, et al. Discovering traffic bottlenecks in an urban network by spatiotemporal data mining on location-based services. IEEE Transactions on Intelligent Transportation Systems, 2011, 12(4): 1047-1056.

[48] Kumaran R S, Parkavi R, Jayasudha M, et al. Secure and Location Based Energy Efficient Protocol for Wireless Sensor Networks. International Conference on Smart Technologies and Systems for Next Generation Computing (ICSTSN), IEEE, 2023: 1-5.

[49] Frith J, Saker M. It is all about location: Smartphones and tracking the spread of COVID-19. Social Media + Society, 2020, 6(3): 2056305120948257.

[50] Schmidtke H R. Location-aware systems or location-based services: a survey with applications to CoViD-19 contact tracking. Journal of Reliable Intelligent Environments, 2020, 6(4): 191-214.

[51] Raza A, Safdar M, Zhong M, et al. Analyzing Spatial Location Preference of Urban Activities with Mode-Dependent Accessibility Using Integrated Land Use-Transport Models. Land, 2022, 11(8): 1139.

[52] Cheng Z, Caverlee J, Kamath K Y, et al. Toward traffic-driven location-based web search. Proceedings of the 20th ACM international conference on Information and knowledge management. 2011: 805-814.

[53] Wu L, Wei X, Meng L, et al. Privacy-preserving location-based traffic density monitoring. Connection Science, 2022, 34(1): 874-894.

[54] Kreutmayr S, Storch D J, Niederle S, et al. Time-Dependent and Location-Based Analysis of Power Consumption at Public Charging Stations in Urban Areas. 2021.

[55] Celik Turkoglu D, Erol Genevois M. A comparative survey of service facility location problems. Annals of Operations Research, 2020, 292: 399-468.

[56] Maddikunta P K R, Gadekallu T R, Al-Ahmari A, et al. Location based business recommendation using spatial demand. Sustainability, 2020, 12(10): 4124.

[57] Zeng Q, Zhong M, Zhu Y, et al. Business location planning based on a novel geo-social influence diffusion model. Information Sciences, 2021, 559: 61-74.

[58] Zhao G, Lou P, Qian X, et al. Personalized location recommendation by fusing sentimental and spatial context. Knowledge-Based Systems, 2020, 196: 105849.

[59] Gao K, Yang X, Wu C, et al. Exploiting location-based context for poi recommendation when traveling to a new region. IEEE Access, 2020, 8: 52404-52412.

[60] Cliquet G, Baray J. Location-Based Marketing: Geomarketing and Geolocation. John Wiley & Sons, 2020.

[61] Luo M, Li G, Chen X. Competitive location-based mobile coupon targeting strategy. Journal of Retailing and Consumer Services, 2021, 58: 102313.

[62] Banerjee S, Xu S, Johnson S D. How does location based marketing affect mobile retail revenues? The complex interplay of delivery tactic, interface mobility and user privacy. Journal of Business Research, 2021, 130: 398-404.

[63] Maddikunta P K R, Gadekallu T R, Al-Ahmari A, et al. Location based business recommendation using spatial demand. Sustainability, 2020, 12(10): 4124.

[64] Batuwanthudawa B I, Jayasena K P N. Real-time location based augmented reality advertising platform. International Conference on Advancements in Computing (ICAC). IEEE, 2020, 1: 174-179.

[65] Wu Z, Li G, Shen S, et al. Constructing dummy query sequences to protect location privacy and query privacy in location-based services. World Wide Web, 2021, 24: 25-49.

[66] Jiang H, Li J, Zhao P, et al. Location privacy-preserving mechanisms in location-based services: A comprehensive survey. ACM Computing Surveys (CSUR), 2021, 54(1): 1-36.

[67] Xu C, Luo L, Ding Y, et al. Personalized location privacy protection for location-based services in vehicular networks. IEEE Wireless Communications Letters, 2020, 9(10): 1633-1637.

[68] Cui Y, Gao F, Li W, et al. Cache-based privacy-preserving solution for location and content protection in location-based services. Sensors, 2020, 20(16): 4651.

[69] Nisha N, Natgunanathan I, Gao S, et al. A novel privacy protection scheme for location-based services using collaborative caching. Computer Networks, 2022, 213: 109107.

[70] Perusco L, Michael K. Control, trust, privacy, and security: evaluating location-based services. IEEE Technology and society magazine, 2007, 26(1): 4-16.

[71] Rodriguez-Priego N, Porcu L, Kitchen P J. Sharing but caring: Location based mobile applications (LBMA) and privacy protection motivation. Journal of Business Research, 2022, 140: 546-555.

[72] Shokri R, Theodorakopoulos G, Le Boudec J Y, et al. Quantifying location privacy. 2011 IEEE symposium on security and privacy. IEEE, 2011: 247-262.

[73] Agarwal R, Hussain M. Generic framework for privacy preservation in cyber-physical systems. Progress in Advanced Computing and Intelligent Engineering, Advances in Intelligent Systems and Computing, 2021, 257-266.

[74] Ashibani Y, Mahmoud Q H. Cyber physical systems security: Analysis, challenges and solutions. Computers & Security, 2017, 68: 81-97.

[75] https://www.sohu.com/a/388842812_135032

[76] Chang V, Mou Y Q, Xu Q A. The ethical issues of location-based services on big data and IoT. Modern Industrial IoT, Big Data and Supply Chain. Springer, 2021: 195-205.

[77] Shokri R, Freudiger J, Jadliwala M, et al. A distortion-based metric for location privacy. Proceedings of the 8th ACM Workshop on Privacy in the Electronic Society. 2009: 21-30.

[78] Wang L, Zhang D, Yang D, et al. Sparse mobile crowdsensing with differential and distortion location privacy. IEEE Transactions on Information Forensics and Security, 2020, 15: 2735-2749.

[79] Kido H, Yanagisawa Y, Satoh T. Protection of location privacy using dummies for location-based services. International Conference on Data Engineering Workshops (ICDEW'05). IEEE, 2005: 1248-1252.

[80] Suzuki A, Iwata M, Arase Y, et al. A user location anonymization method for location based services in a real environment. Proceedings of the 18th SIGSPATIAL International Conference on Advances in Geographic Information Systems, 2010: 398-401.

[81] Kato R, Iwata M, Hara T, et al. A dummy-based anonymization method based on user trajectory with pauses. Proceedings of the 20th International Conference on Advances in Geographic Information Systems, Redondo, 2012, 249–258.

[82] Dwork C. Differential privacy. In the Proceedings of the 33rd International Colloquium on Automata, Languages and Programming, 2006, 1-12.

[83] Dwork C. Differential privacy: a survey of results. In the Proceedings of the International Conference on Theory and Applications of Models of Computation, 2008, 1-19.

[84] Kim J W, Edemacu K, Kim J S, et al. A survey of differential privacy-based techniques and their applicability to location-based services. Computers & Security, 2021, 111: 102464.

[85] Gruteser M, Grunwald D. Anonymous usage of location-based services through spatial and temporal cloaking. Proceedings of the 1st International Conference on Mobile Systems, Applications and Services, 2003, 31-42.

[86] Hwang R H, Hsueh Y L, Chung H W. A novel time-obfuscated algorithm for trajectory privacy protection. IEEE Transactions on Services Computing, 2013, 7(2): 126-139.

[87] De Montjoye Y A, Hidalgo C A, Verleysen M, et al. Unique in the crowd: The privacy bounds of human mobility. Scientific Reports, 2013, 3(1): 1-5.

[88] Eddy S R. Hidden Markov Models. Current Opinion in Structural Biology, 1996, 6(3): 361-365.

[89] Mokbel M F, Chow C Y, Aref W G. The new casper: Query processing for location services without compromising privacy. VLDB. 2006, 6: 763-774.

[90] Gotz M, Nath S, Gehrke J. Maskit: Privately releasing user context streams for personalized mobile applications. Proceedings of the 2012 ACM SIGMOD International Conference on Management of Data, 2012: 289-300.

[91] Komishani E G, Abadi M, Deldar F. PPTD: Preserving personalized privacy in trajectory data publishing by sensitive attribute generalization and trajectory local suppression. Knowledge-Based Systems, 2016, 94: 43-59.

[92] Terrovitis M, Poulis G, Mamoulis N, et al. Local suppression and splitting techniques for privacy-preserving publication of trajectories. IEEE Transactions on Knowledge and Data Engineering, 2017, 29(7): 1466-1479.

[93] Lin C Y. Suppression techniques for privacy-preserving trajectory data publishing. Knowledge-Based Systems, 2020, 206:106354.

[94] Karimi R, Kalantari M. Enhancing security and confidentiality in location-based data encryption algorithms. Fourth International Conference on the Applications of Digital Information and Web Technologies, IEEE, 2011: 30-35.

[95] Chen G, Zhao J, Jin Y, et al. Certificateless deniable authenticated encryption for location-based privacy protection. IEEE Access, 2019, 7: 101704-101717.

[96] Peng K. Anonymous communication networks: Protecting Privacy on the Web. CRC Press, 2014.

[97] Mittal P, Olumofin F, Troncoso C, et al. PIR-Tor: Scalable Anonymous Communication Using Private Information Retrieval. 20th USENIX Security Symposium, 2011.

[98] Du W, Atallah M J. Secure multi-party computation problems and their applications: a review and open problems. Proceedings of the 2001 Workshop on New Security Paradigms, 2001: 13-22.

[99] Zhao C, Zhao S, Zhao M, et al. Secure multi-party computation: theory, practice and applications. Information Sciences, 2019, 476: 357-372.

[100] Acar A, Aksu H, Uluagac A S, et al. A survey on homomorphic encryption schemes: Theory and implementation. ACM Computing Surveys, 2018, 51(4): 1-35.

[101] Naehrig M, Lauter K, Vaikuntanathan V. Can homomorphic encryption be practical? Proceedings of the 3rd ACM Workshop on Cloud Computing Security Workshop, 2011: 113-124.

[102] Fan J, Vercauteren F. Somewhat practical fully homomorphic encryption. Cryptology ePrint Archive, 2012.

[103] Chor B, Kushilevitz E, Goldreich O, et al. Private information retrieval. Journal of the ACM, 1998, 45(6): 965-981.

[104] Yekhanin S. Private information retrieval. Communications of the ACM, 2010, 53(4): 68-73.

[105] Li D R, Shao Z F, Yu W B, et al. Public epidemic prevention and control services based on big data of spatiotemporal location make cities more smart. Geomatics and Information Science of Wuhan University, 2020, 45(4): 475-487, 556.

[106] Guo Y, Zhang Y, Boulaksil Y, et al. Multi-dimensional spatiotemporal demand forecasting and service vehicle dispatching for online car-hailing platforms. International Journal of Production Research, 2022, 60(6): 1832-1853.

[107] Terroso-Saenz F, Munoz A. Nation-wide human mobility prediction based on graph neural networks. Applied Intelligence, 2022, 52(4): 4144-4160.

[108] Hasan I, Dhawan P, Rizvi S A M, et al. Data analytics and knowledge management approach for COVID-19 prediction and control. International Journal of Information Technology, 2023, 15(2): 937-954.

[109] Ni L, Tian F, Ni Q, et al. An anonymous entropy-based location privacy protection scheme in mobile social networks. EURASIP Journal on Wireless Communications and Networking, 2019, 1: 93-96.

[110] Wang Y, Zuo K, Liu R, et al. Dynamic pseudonym semantic-location privacy protection based on continuous query for road network. International Journal of Network Security, 2021, 23: 642-649.

[111] Shen X Y, Wang L C, Pei Q Q, et al. Location privacy-preserving in online taxi-hailing services. Peer-to-Peer Networking and Applications, 2020, 1-13.

[112] Liu H Y, Zhang S W, Li M L, et al. An effective location privacy-preserving k-anonymity scheme in location based services. IEEE International Conference on Electronic Technology, Communication and Information, 2021, 24-29.

[113] Terrovitis M, Poulis G, Mamoulis N, et al. Local suppression and splitting techniques for privacy-preserving publication of trajectories. IEEE Transactions on Knowledge and Data Engineering, 2017, 29(7): 1466-1479.

[114] Chen R, Fung B C M, Mohammed N, et al. Privacy-preserving trajectory data publishing by local suppression. Information Sciences, 2013, 231: 83-97.

[115] Kaur J, Agrawal A, Khan R A. Encryfuscation: A model for preserving data and location privacy in fog based IoT scenario. Journal of King Saud University - Computer and Information Sciences, 2022, 34(9): 6808-6817.

[116] Lv Z, Qiao L, Hossain M S, et al. Analysis of using blockchain to protect the privacy of drone big data. IEEE Network, 2021, 35(1): 44-49.

[117] Zhao Y, Yuan D, Du J T, et al. Geo-ellipse-indistinguishability: community-aware location privacy protection for directional distribution. IEEE Transactions on Knowledge and Data Engineering, 2022.

[118] Zhao X D, Pi D C, Chen J F. Novel trajectory privacy-preserving method based on clustering using differential privacy. Expert Systems with Applications, 2020, 149: 113241.

[119] Min M H, Wang W H, Liang X, et al. Reinforcement learning-based sensitive semantic location privacy protection for VANETs. China Communications, 2021, 18(6): 244-260.

[120] Yang M M, Zhu T Q, Xiang Y, et al. Density-based location preservation for mobile crowdsensing with differential privacy. IEEE Access, 2018, 6: 14779-14789.

[121] Yan Y, Hao X H, Zhang L X. Hierarchical differential privacy hybrid decomposition algorithm for location big data. Cluster Computing-the Journal of Networks Software Tools and Application, 2019, 22(4): 9269-9280.

[122] Yan Y, Gao X, Mahmood A, et al. Differential private spatial decomposition and location publishing based on unbalanced quadtree partition algorithm. IEEE Access, 2020, 8(1): 104775-104787.

[123] Rodriguez K M, Bossy M, Maftei R, et al. New spatial decomposition method for accurate, mesh-independent agglomeration predictions in particle-laden flows. Applied Mathematical Modelling, 2021, 90: 582-614.

[124] Wei J H, Lin Y P, Yao X, et al. Differential privacy-based location protection in spatial crowdsourcing. IEEE Transactions on Services Computing, 2022, 15(1): 45-58.

[125] Onadi N, Kamandi A, Shabankhah M, et al. SW-DBSCAN: A grid-based DBSCAN algorithm for large datasets. The 6th International Conference on Web Research, 2020, 139-145.

[126] Xu H, Yao S, Li Q. An improved K-means clustering algorithm. IEEE 5th International Symposium on Smart and Wireless Systems within the Conferences on Intelligent Data Acquisition and Advanced Computing Systems, 2020, 1-5.

[127] Cai L, Wang H Y, Jiang F, et al. A new clustering mining algorithm for multi-source imbalanced location data. Information Sciences, 2022, 584: 50-64.

[128] Yan Y, Sun Z C, Mahmood A, et al. Achieving differential privacy publishing of location-based statistical data using grid clustering. ISPRS International Journal of Geo-Information, 2022, 11(7): 404.

[129] Fan L Y, Xiong L. An adaptive approach to real-time aggregate monitoring with differential privacy. IEEE Transactions on Knowledge & Data Engineering, 2014, 26(9): 1.

[130] Yan Y, Zhang L X, Sheng Q Z, et al. Dynamic release of big location data based on adaptive sampling and differential privacy. IEEE Access, 2019, 7: 164962-164974.

[131] Ma Z, Zhang T, Liu X M, et al. Real-time privacy-preserving data release over vehicle trajectory. IEEE Transactions on Vehicular Technology, 2019, 68(8): 8091-8102.

[132] Iqbal W, Berral J L, Carrera D. Adaptive sliding windows for improved estimation of data center resource utilization. Future Generation Computer Systems, 2020, 104: 212-224.

[133] Ahsani S, Sanati M Y, Mansoorizadeh M. Improvement of CluStream algorithm using sliding window for the clustering of data streams. The 11th International Conference on Computer Engineering and Knowledge, 2021, 434-440.

[134] Sayed D, Rady S, Aref M. Enhancing CluStream algorithm for clustering big data streaming over sliding window. The 12th International Conference on Electrical Engineering, 2020, 108-114.

[135] Dwork C, McSherry F, Nissim K, et al. Calibrating noise to sensitivity in private data analysis. Theory of Cryptography: Third Theory of Cryptography Conference, 2006, 265-284.

[136] McSherry F D. Privacy integrated queries: an extensible platform for privacy-preserving data analysis. Proceedings of the 2009 ACM SIGMOD International Conference on Management of data, 2009, 19-30.

[137] Kellaris G, Papadopoulos S, Xiao X, et al. Differentially private event sequences over infinite streams. Proceedings of the VLDB Endowment, 2014, 7(12): 1155-1166.

[138] Ali A, Zhu Y, Zakarya M. A data aggregation based approach to exploit dynamic spatio-temporal correlations for citywide crowd flows prediction in fog computing. Multimedia Tools and Applications, 2021, 1-33.

[139] Lu Y, Wang L Z. Mining traffic congestion propagation patterns based on spatio-temporal co-location patterns. Evolutionary Intelligence, 2020, 13(2): 221-233.

[140] Dwork C, Naor M, Pitassi T, et al. Differential privacy under continual observation. Proceedings of the Annual ACM Symposium on Theory of Computing, 2010, 715-724.

[141] http://www.nyc.gov/html/tlc/html/about/trip_record_data.shtml

[142] Kasiviswanathan S P, Lee H K, Nissim K, et al. What can we learn privately? Proceedings of the 49th Annual IEEE Symp. on Foundations of Computer Science, 2008, 531-540.

[143] Duchi J C, Jordan M I, Wainwright M J. Local privacy and statistical minimax rates. Proceedings of the 54th Annual IEEE Symp. On Foundations of Computer Science, 2013, 429-438.

[144] Zhang Y B, Zhang Q Y, Yan Y, et al. A k-anonymous location privacy protection method of polygon based on density distribution. International Journal of Network Security, 2021, 23(1): 57-66.

[145] Sun G, Cai S, Yu H, et al. Location privacy preservation for mobile users in location-based services. IEEE Access, 2019, 7: 87425-87438.

[146] Peng W, Ma D, Song C, et al. A K-Anonymous location privacy-preserving scheme for mobile terminals. EAI Endorsed Transactions on e-Learning, 2023, 9.

[147] Xu X, Chen H, Xie L. A location privacy preservation method based on dummy locations in Internet of vehicles. Applied Sciences, 2021, 11(10): 4594.

[148] Zhang X J, Fu N, Meng X F et al. Towards Spatial Range Queries Under Local Differential Privacy. Journal of Computer Research and Development, 2020, 57(4): 847-858.

[149] Zhu L, Hong H, Xie M. A novel protection method of continuous location sharing based on local differential privacy and conditional random field. Algorithms and Architectures for Parallel Processing: 21st International Conference, ICA3PP 2021, Virtual Event, December 3-5, 2021, Proceedings, Part I. Cham: Springer International Publishing, 2022: 710-725.

[150] Errounda F Z, Liu Y. Collective location statistics release with local differential privacy. Future Generation Computer Systems, 2021, 124: 174-186.

[151] Yan Y, Dong Z Y, Xu F, et al. Local differential privacy location protection method with Hilbert encoding. Journal of Xidian University, 2023, 50(02): 148-161.

[152] Yang Z, Wang R, Wu D, et al. Local trajectory privacy protection in 5G enabled industrial intelligent logistics. IEEE Transactions on Industrial Informatics, 2021, 18(4): 2868-2876.

[153] Hong D, Jung W, Shim K. Collecting geospatial data with local differential privacy for personalized services. IEEE 37th International Conference on Data Engineering, 2021, 2237-2242.

[154] Wang H, Hong H, Xiong L, et al. L-srr: Local differential privacy for location-based services with staircase randomized response. Proceedings of the 2022

ACM SIGSAC Conference on Computer and Communications Security, 2022, 2809-2823.

[155] Hong D, Jung W, Shim K. Collecting geospatial data under local differential privacy with improving frequency estimation. IEEE Transactions on Knowledge and Data Engineering, 2022, DOI: 10.1109/TKDE.2022.3181049.

[156] Warner S L. Randomized response: A survey technique for eliminating evasive answer bias. Journal of the American Statistical Association, 1965, 60(309): 63-69.

[157] Zhou Y H, Lu L F, Wu Z Q. Study on utility optimization for randomized response mechanism. Journal on Communications, 2019, 40(06): 74-81.

[158] Wang J, Wang F, Li H T. Differential privacy location protection scheme based on Hilbert curve. Security and Communication Networks, 2021, 12.

[159] Zhao X G, Li Y H, Yuan Y, et al. LDPart: effective location-record data publication via local differential privay. IEEE Access, 2019, 7: 31435-31445.

[160] http://www.infochimps.com/datasets/storage-facilities-by-landmarks

[161] Yang D Q, Zhang D Q, Zheng V W, et al. Modeling user activity preference by leveraging user spatial temporal characteristics in LBSNs. IEEE Transactions on Systems Man and Cybernetics, 2014, 45(1): 129-142.

[162] Andres M E, Bordenabe N E, Chatzikokolakis K, et al. Geo-indistinguishability: Differential privacy for location-based systems. Proceedings of the 2013 ACM SIGSAC Conference on Computer & Communications Security. 2013: 901-914.

[163] Takagi S, Cao Y, Asano Y, et al. Geo-graph-indistinguishability: Protecting location privacy for LBS over road networks. IFIP Annual Conference on Data and Applications Security and Privacy, 2019, 143-163.

[164] Chatzikokolakis K, Palamidessi C, Stronati M. Location privacy via geo-indistinguishability. ACM Siglog News, 2015, 2(3): 46-69.

[165] Yu L, Liu L, Pu C. Dynamic differential location privacy with personalized error bounds. NDSS, 2017.

[166] Al-Dhubhani R, Cazalas J M. An adaptive geo-indistinguishability mechanism for continuous LBS queries. Wireless Networks, 2018, 24(8): 3221-3239.

[167] Hua J Y, Tong W, Xu F Y, et al. A geo-indistinguishable location perturbation mechanism for location-based services supporting frequent queries. IEEE Transactions on Information Forensics and Security, 2017, 13(5): 1155-1168.

[168] Qiu C, Squicciarini A, Pang C, et al. Location privacy protection in vehicle-based spatial crowdsourcing via geo-indistinguishability. IEEE Transactions on Mobile Computing, 2020.

[169] Arain Q A, Memon I, Deng Z, et al. Location monitoring approach: multiple mix-zones with location privacy protection based on traffic flow over road networks. Multimedia Tools and Applications, 2018, 77(5): 5563-5607.

[170] Luo H W, Zhang H M, Long S G, et al. Enhancing frequent location privacy-preserving strategy based on geo-Indistinguishability. Multimedia Tools and Applications, 2021, 80(14): 21823-21841.

[171] Xiong P, Li G R, Ren W, et al. LOPO: A location privacy-preserving path optimization scheme for spatial crowdsourcing. Journal of Ambient Intelligence and Humanized Computing, 2021, 1-16.

[172] Xiao Z, Xu J L, Meng X F. p-sensitivity: A semantic privacy-protection model for location-based services. The Ninth International Conference on Mobile Data Management Workshops, MDMW, 2008, 47-54.

[173] Lee B, Oh J, Yu H, et al. Protecting location privacy using location semantics. Proceedings of the 17th ACM SIGKDD International Conference on Knowledge Discovery and Data Mining, 2011, 1289-1297.

[174] Agir B, Huguenin K, Hengartner U, et al. On the privacy implications of location semantics. Proceedings on Privacy Enhancing Technologies, 2016.

[175] Li Y H, Cao X, Yuan Y, et al. PrivSem: Protecting location privacy using semantic and differential privacy. World Wide Web, 2019, 22(6): 2407-2436.

[176] Wang J, Wang C, Ma J, et al. Dummy location selection algorithm based on location semantics and query probability. Journal on Communications, 2020, 41(3): 53.

[177] Kuang L, Wang Y, Zheng X S, et al. Using location semantics to realize personalized road network location privacy protection. EURASIP Journal on Wireless Communications and Networking, 2020, 1, 1-16.

[178] Bostanipour B, Theodorakopoulos G. Joint obfuscation of location and its semantic information for privacy protection. Computers & Security, 2021, 107, 102310.

[179] Min M H, Wang W Q, Xiao L, et al. Reinforcement learning-based sensitive semantic location privacy protection for VANETs. China Communications, 2021, 18(6): 244-260.

[180] Xiao Y L, Xiao L, Lu X Z, et al. Deep-reinforcement-learning-based user profile perturbation for privacy-aware recommendation. IEEE Internet of Things Journal, 2020, 8(6): 4560-4568.

[181] Damiani M L, Bertino E, Silvestri C. The PROBE Framework for the personalized cloaking of private locations. Transaction in Data Privacy, 2010, 3(2): 123-148.

[182] Yang D, Zhang D, Zheng V, et al. Modeling user activity preference by leveraging user spatial temporal characteristics in LBSNs. IEEE Trans. Syst. Man Cybern. Syst. 2014, 45, 129-142.

[183] Kairouz P, Oh S, Viswanath P. Extremal mechanisms for local differential privacy. Journal of Machine Learning Research, 2016, 17(17): 1–51.

[184] Alvim M S, Chatzikokolakis K, Palamidessi C, et al. Metric-based local differential privacy for statistical applications. 2018.DOI:10.48550/arXiv.1805.01456.

[185] Gursoy M E, Tamersoy A, Truex S, et al. Secure and utility-aware data collection with condensed local differential privacy. IEEE Transactions on Dependable and Secure Computing, 2019.

[186] Li F, Li H, Niu B, et al. Privacy computing: concept, computing framework, and future development trends. Engineering, 2019, 1179-1192.

[187] Grassi L, Khovratovich D, Rechberger C, et al. Poseidon: A new hash function for Zero-Knowledge proof systems. 30th USENIX Security Symposium, 2021, 519-535.

[188] Li L, Fan Y, Tse M, et al. A review of applications in federated learning. Computers & Industrial Engineering, 2020, 149: 106854.

[189] Zhang C, Xie Y, Bai H, et al. A survey on federated learning. Knowledge-Based Systems, 2021, 216: 106775.

[190] Nieminen R, J Jarvinen K. Practical privacy-preserving indoor localization based on secure two-party computation. IEEE Transactions on Mobile Computing, 2020, 20(9): 2877-2890.

[191] Li S, Zhao S, Min G, et al. Lightweight privacy-preserving scheme using homomorphic encryption in industrial internet of things. IEEE Internet of Things Journal, 2021, 9(16): 14542-14550.

[192] Li B, Liang R, Zhou W, et al. LBS meets blockchain: An efficient method with security preserving trust in SAGIN. IEEE Internet of Things Journal, 2021, 9(8): 5932-5942.

[193] Qi Z, Chen W. Location privacy protection of IoV based on blockchain and K-anonymity technology. The 6th International Conference on Electronics Technology, 2023, 15-21.

Printed in the United States
by Baker & Taylor Publisher Services